THE MANAGER'S POCKET GUIDE TO

 ## STRATEGIC AND BUSINESS PLANNING

THE SYSTEMS THINKING APPROACH

How to use The Systems Thinking Approach as a guide to more effective problem solving, decision making, and change management in our daily lives.

by *Stephen G. Haines*
President and Founder of the
Centre for Strategic Management

HRD PRESS
Amherst, Massachusetts

Published by:
HRD Press
22 Amherst Road
1-800-822-2801
(U.S. and Canada)
1-413-253-3488
1-413-253-3490 (Fax)
www.hrdpress.com

ISBN 0-87425-515-5

Cover design by Eileen Klockars
Production services by Michele Anctil
Editorial services by Suzanne Bay

Printed in Canada

How to reach the author:

Stephen G. Haines
Centre for Strategic Management
1420 Monitor Road
San Diego, CA 92110-1545
E-mail: Csmintl@san.rr.com
Website: Csmintl.com
Telephone: (619) 275-6528
Fax: (619) 275-0324

TABLE OF CONTENTS

— OVERVIEW AND INTRODUCTION—

Thinking Backwards.. 1

— APPLICATIONS —

Chapter I
Three Seemingly Simple Elements... 5

Chapter II
The ABCs of Strategic Management
    (Planning and Change).. 19

Chapter III
Phase $\boxed{A}$: Ideal-Future Vision.. 29

Chapter IV
Phase $\boxed{B}$: Key Success Factors 51

Chapter V
Phase $\boxed{C}$: From Assessment to Strategy.................................... 55

Chapter VI
Phase $\boxed{D}$: Implementation... 93

Chapter VII
How to Get Started 125

— CONCLUSION —

Chapter VIII
Summary: Recap of Key Points and Checklists...................... 133

Chapter IX
Facilitation Tips... 167

Index 169
About the Author 175

Insanity and Change

Insanity . . .
is doing the same things in the same way and expecting
different results.

Change . . .
Effective change takes two to five years, even with
concentrated and continual actions.

—*Stephen G. Haines (1992)*

THE ABCs OF STRATEGIC MANAGEMENT

Definition:

Strategic Planning

+

Strategic Change Management

Three Goals:

#1 Develop Strategic/Business Plans and Document(s)

#2 Ensure their Successful Implementation and Change

#3 Build and Sustain High Performance

Three Main Premises:

#1 Planning/Change Management are a *Primary* Part of Leadership and Management

#2 People Support What They Help Create

#3 Use Systems Thinking; Focus on Outcomes; *Serve the Customer.*

Four Phases of Strategic Management:

A
Vision
Values

B
Measures
Feedback

C
Assessment
Strategies

D
Actions
Change

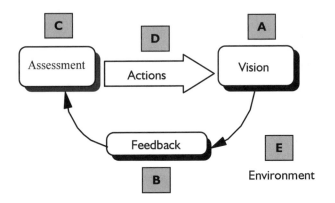

– Results –

The Systems Thinking Approach to Creating a Customer-Focused, High-Performance Learning Organization

Thinking Backwards

Everyone understands that rapid and tumultuous change is about the only thing we can predict for the new millennium. Perhaps at no other time have the prospects seemed so dazzling, nor the possible pitfalls so numerous and deep.

In the Industrial Age, public and private enterprises built their futures by incrementally expanding technologies, assumptions, and day-to-day operations. In today's global Information Age, building on the present is not enough, by a long shot.

Worldwide markets and the instant global communications of the Internet and 24-hour cable news broadcasts are multiplying the opportunities available to every entrepreneur, not to mention consumers and employees. Today, organizations must keep pace with changes in their environment and overhaul current businesses, programs, and operations.

They must completely reinvent their future vision and then begin thinking backwards to this future with the strategies and actions needed to achieve their goals. They must also react to the changing values and demands of customers and employees, as the intangible goals of personal growth and fulfillment become as important as material needs.

The danger of this dynamic "new reality" is that corporations and governmental bureaucracies can be swallowed up before they know what is happening to them. The experiences of former Communist Bloc nations are a lesson to us all.

Rapid change has taken its toll in the West, too. Thirty-three percent of the firms on the 1970 "Fortune 500" list have vanished. San Diego alone has seen the demise of its five biggest financial services firms. In a troubled and rapidly changing economy, the mortality rate for firms that refuse to change goes higher and higher, while Information Age start-ups create young millionaires many times over.

It is within this global sea change that new ways to do planning are emerging: the Systems Thinking Approach, based on years of rigorous scientific work by General Systems theorists and augmented by extensive research by the author, has led to the reinvention and creation of a new way to plan and create one's ideal future. The chaos and complexity in today's world demand that we change our approach; the key is *thinking backwards to the future.* It will create an ABC-like elegant simplicity that can be used by first time supervisors all the way up to senior executives.

How can the modern organization cope with the future's appetite for the slow-footed? Should we all hire fortune-tellers to help us? Should we hang onto every word uttered by Peters, Senge, and the century's other gurus? Or should we just hunker down and wait for the environment to stabilize?

My own experience and research in a wide variety of public and private organizations has convinced me that the only way to guarantee the future you desire is to design and pursue a *Customer-Focused "Ideal Vision,"* using the Systems Thinking Approach. In this guide we will discuss how to achieve this "Ideal" through this unique and integrated perspective, using the *three primary goals* of any Strategic Management System:

> **GOAL #1:** Develop a Strategic Plan/Document
>
> **GOAL #2:** Ensure its successful Implementation
>
> **GOAL #3:** Build and sustain High Performance over the long term

In order to show you how we assist private and public organizations in achieving these three goals, we have organized this Pocket Guide into six main sections, as follows:

1. The first section covers our underlying assumptions (**Three Seemingly Simple Elements**) and the benefits our clients have achieved using the Systems Thinking Approach detailed here.

2. The second section briefly shows our copyrighted **"Strategic Management System"** in a logical (yet circular) way. This should give you a clear picture of our approach, which uses our two goals mentioned and three Seemingly Simple Elements.

3. Thirdly, we will discuss the **ABCs of Strategic Management** based on the **Systems Thinking Approach** (and the science of General Systems Theory).

4. Fourth, we will discuss in detail the **first eight steps of strategic planning** within three phases.

5. Then we will finish the discussion of the last two steps of the D Phase of Strategic Change, thus completing the **entire Strategic Management Process.**

6. Lastly, we will show you **how to get started** on your own journey toward creating a customer-focused, high-performance learning organization.

Keep in mind that we will discuss this Strategic Management System within the sequence of the three goals: strategic planning; successful strategic change management; and sustaining high performance.

**APPLICATIONS**

I. Three Seemingly Simple Elements

It is most important that you first get an understanding of the *Three Seemingly Simple Elements that form the basis for our Systems Thinking Approach to transform and reinvent strategic management (planning and change) from its checkered past.* For example, the number of corporate-planning jobs is rapidly decreasing. Planners have become an endangered species. Planning itself, however, has increased as senior executives try to make sense out of today's turbulent and revolutionary times. *Hence the need to reinvent planning and change management, and to do it wisely and effectively. The three simple elements described below* will help you in your change effort.

The Systems Thinking Approach provides some very clear **STRATEGIC ANSWERS** to the questions asked of organizations who want to be successful in the long-term. However, there is no single answer—not even the reliance on Total Quality Management (TQM) or its successors, Business Reengineering, value chain management, or any other single management fad.

The closest we will come to finding a Holy Grail is what we find in Three Seemingly Simple Elements, described here:

SEEMINGLY SIMPLE ELEMENT #1

Planning and Change are a part of Management and Leadership

An organization or team embarking on a strategic or business planning and change process must first ask itself: Is strategic planning:

(1) an event?
(2) a process?
(3) a change in our roles?
(4) a change in the way we run our business day-to-day?

While the complete answer is "all of the above," ***strategic and business planning must be transformed into strategic management*** and culminate in a significant change in the way we do business. This is a key difference between our model and most others, which suffer from the often-fatal "SPOTS" Syndrome (Strategic Plans On Top Shelves, gathering dust). ***This is actually Strategic Answer #1: achieving our three goals by instituting a yearly Strategic Management Cycle and System.*** Strategic business plans are the blueprints; senior managers and department heads must change their behaviors and that of others to fill in the implementation details, based on a strategic perspective and a system.

Our model focuses on the arduous implementation of real change—a change in all the diverse human behaviors that collectively make up an organization's culture. Changing human behavior in an entire firm or business unit to one in which the customer is paramount requires the continual reinforcement of new behaviors. You must counter the natural human tendency to revert back to the familiar behaviors and habits of the past.

Thus, it cannot be stressed too early that strategic and business planning and the implementation/change processes must be championed over the long haul by a "monomaniac with a mission"—the CEO or division/department's top executive.

6

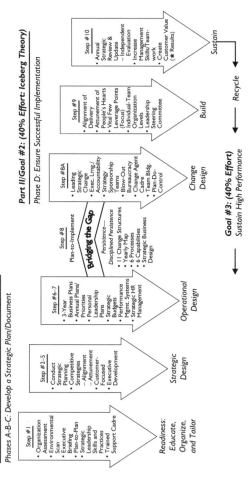

CREATING CUSTOMER VALUE

A three-part "Strategic Management Systems" Solution

Part I/Goal #1: (20% Effort: Cascade of Planning)

Phases A-B-C: Develop a Strategic Plan/Document

Step #1
- Organization Assessment
- Environmental Scan
- Executive Briefing
- Plan-to-Plan
- Strategic Leadership Skills and Practices
- Trained Support Cadre

Readiness: Educate, Organize, and Tailor

Step #2-5
- Conduct Strategic Planning
- Competitive Strategies
  – Alignment
  – Attunement
- Customer-Focused
- Executive Development

Strategic Design

Step #6-7
- 3-Year Business Plans
- Annual Planning/ Priorities
- Personal Leadership Plans
- Strategic Budgets
- Performance Mgmt. Systems
- Strategic HR Management

Operational Design

Step #8
Plan-to-Implement

Bridging the Gap

Persistence–
Disciplined Persistence
- 11 Change Structures
- Yearly Map
- 6 Processes
- 6 Capabilities
- Strategic Business Design

Part II/Goal #2: (40% Effort: Iceberg Theory)

Phase D: Ensure Successful Implementation

Step #8A
- Leading Strategic Change
- Exec. Lng./ Accountability
- Strategy Sponsorship Teams
- Blow-Out Bureaucracy
- Change Agent Cadre
- Team Bldg.
- Plan-Do-Control

Change Design

Step #9
- Alignment of Delivery
- Attunement of People's Hearts
- Vital Few Leverage Points (Focus)
- Individual-Team Organization Levels
- Leadership Steering Committee

Build

Step #10
- Annual Strategic Review & Update
  – Independent Evaluation
- Increase Management Skills/Team-work
- Create Customer Value (★ Results)

Sustain

Recycle

Goal #3: (40% Effort)
Sustain High Performance

7

To achieve this, you must completely revamp your current management system. Our reinvented Strategic and Business Planning Model implements key concepts not found collectively in any other strategic planning/strategic change models.

THE GOALS

1. DEVELOP YOUR STRATEGIC AND/OR BUSINESS PLAN.

Begin with Plan-to-Plan. (Step 1)

Our "plan-to-plan" step #1 concept educates, organizes, and tailors the strategic or business planning process to the organization's specific needs. It involves key stake-holders in the "Parallel Process" concept, and clarifies top executive roles in leading, developing, and owning the strategic plan. Alternatives to this approach are **Strategic Planning Quick, Micro Strategic Planning,** or **Three-Year Business Planning** processes for smaller organizations or divisions/major support departments, or when a fast jump-start implementation is critical during cost cutting, turnarounds, mergers, and similar events.

Conduct Actual Strategic Planning. (Steps 2–5)

The concept of an "Ideal-Future Vision" is the starting point for a Systems Thinking Strategic Management Process that helps clarify and implement tough choices. It focuses the organization and its core strategies on satisfying the customer—your only outcome or reason for existence.

These steps make up the blueprint for strategic design. They cover the development of organizational values

8

or "culture," the measurement of quantifiable outcome measures, and goals or Key Success Factors.

Lastly, they include the development of a Current-State Assessment. The core strategies are then developed to fill the gap between the Vision of the Future and what things look like today.

Conduct Operational Planning. (Steps 6–7)

Once strategic planning is completed, an organization must convert these longer-term, strategic decisions into operational ones. In larger organizations, this usually means first developing a three-year Business Plan (Step #6) for each *strategic business unit* or *major program area.* Every major support department (public or private) should have one, also. This includes Finance, HR, Marketing, Legal, and Administrative departments. This Business Planning process looks remarkably like the strategic planning process already described—Plan-to-Plan and a strategic design for the business unit. The main difference is that the Strategic Business Unit or Major Support Department/Program Area (in the Public Sector) must plan **within** the context of the overall larger strategic plan already developed.

Once these three-year Business Plans are developed, you must set up annual plans and strategic budgets that relate to annual actions and priorities (Step #7). Annual plans and budgets must be set within the context of the core strategies already developed. (To set separate department objectives is a big mistake; the objective of each department in every organization should be to support the core strategies of the overall organization.

2. ENSURE SUCCESSFUL IMPLEMENTATION

"Bridging the Gap: Plan-to-Implement

Plan-to-Implement Step #8 is designed to bridge the gap between strategic/business planning and the difficult implementation process. It is an educating, organizing, and tailoring day for the change effort. You must plan for such things as a Strategic Change Leadership Steering Committee, a yearly Comprehensive Map of the implementation process, and the use of cross-functional Strategy Sponsorship Teams. These are all part of the "44 Fail-Safe Mechanisms" that are reviewed during Step #8 to ensure successful Strategic Planning implementation.

Goal #2 also includes *Step #9, Strategy Implementation and Change,* where the actual work and tasks get accomplished. It includes the "Organization-as-a-System" model. In order to make this complex implementation process easier, we have developed a Wheel of Detail comprised of eight key implementation areas and several specific detailed actions used in almost all large-scale, major cultural change efforts.

It also includes the need to (1) create Customer Value in your delivery system, (2) build the necessary Leadership Development System, and (3) institute strategic Human Resource Management practices to create the desired culture to support this delivery.

Both of these needs are crucial to the work of our organization, as well. While we don't consult on all areas of organization development, we do focus on key leverage points.

3. CREATE AND SUSTAIN LONG-TERM HIGH PERFORMANCE

Annual Strategic Review (and Update)

Step #10 includes an Annual Strategic Review and Update, which is usually part of an annual independent financial audit. Strategic and Business Plans are often made for three to seven or more years at a time, but should be formally reviewed and updated yearly to keep pace with change. **Strategic and business plans must be living and breathing documents.** This is the only way to sustain high performance over the long-term.

In summary, this Three-Part/Three-Goal Systems Thinking Approach includes all the elements necessary to design and build a customer-focused, high-performance learning organization. However, our 10-Step Reinvented Strategic Management Planning and Change Model is key. It will be explained in more detail later.

SEEMINGLY SIMPLE ELEMENT #2

"People Support What They Help Create"

In its first year of strategic and business planning, an organization must set in place the necessary strategic planning strategies and *create a critical mass* for the desired changes. A core planning team of eight to fifteen people from your collective leadership should lead the process, do the hard work, and make the decisions.

One crucial planning task is to do a *Parallel Process* (see next page's graphic) that involves the rest of management and key stakeholders in a meaningful way. Gather their input on all draft documents and increase their ownership of the plan. This is the second element; people support what they help create.

➡ For Example

> During the Hayward Unified School District Plan-to-Plan step, the Hayward, California district established a core planning team of 15 people. However, because whatever it does broadly impacts the lives of thousands of families, its work with key stakeholders included over 100 meetings involving 2000+ people.

There's one other component to the involvement of key stakeholders: three-year Business Planning. It is essential that all key line and staff units ultimately develop their own three-year Business Plans under the umbrella of the overall strategic plan. *This need to link levels of planning into one system is often overlooked—a serious omission.*

This brings us to *Strategic Answer #2: the need for Visionary Leadership Practices* that radically differ from those adopted by tyrannical bosses of the past. Leaders at multiple levels, including trainers, coaches, and facilitators, are needed to carry out this Parallel Process during strategic planning, the 3-year Business

Planning, and all strategic management and change processes. Everyone in a managerial position must acquire a wide range of participative management and leadership skills. The two extremes (Feared Bosses and Too Nice Bosses) must be avoided like the plague.

The only advantage an organization has over the long-term is its leadership. Employees become your greatest assets *only if* the leaders allow them to be. If leaders are to have the skills to do, leaders must help them develop a number of different skills and six levels of Natural Leadership competencies, including:

Level #1: Enhancing Your Self-Mastery

Level #2: Building Relationships

Level #3: Building Effective Teams

Level #4: Building Customer-Focused Business Processes

Level #5: Integrating Organizational Outcomes

Level #6: Creating Value for the Customer

This doesn't happen overnight. Leadership is a contemplative art requiring a long-term commitment to it as a separate professional growth opportunity. The ability to lead an entire organization and all its facets and levels effectively is quite a daunting task, requiring a life-long learning perspective.

Thus, it is key for organizations to develop a fully comprehensive "Strategic Leadership Development System" to make certain that each leader develops these six core competencies.

Parallel Process

(INSTEAD OF D.A.D.: Decide, Announce, Defend)

SET UP THE PLANNING COMMUNITY

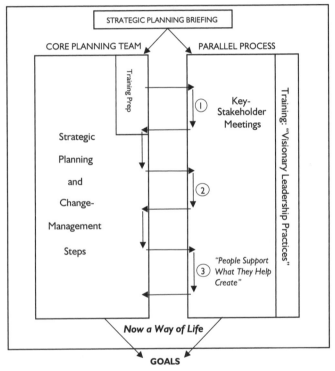

STRATEGIC PLANNING BRIEFING

CORE PLANNING TEAM

PARALLEL PROCESS

Training Prep

Strategic
Planning
and
Change-
Management
Steps

① Key-Stakeholder Meetings

②

③ *"People Support What They Help Create"*

Training: "Visionary Leadership Practices"

Now a Way of Life

GOALS

#1: OWNERSHIP FOR IMPLEMENTATION
#2: BEST POSSIBLE DECISIONS ON FUTURE

SEEMINGLY SIMPLE ELEMENT #3

Use Systems Thinking—Focus on Outcomes: The Customer

The key to the Systems Thinking Approach, as you will see in more detail later, is to focus on your outcomes. Begin with the end in mind and think backwards to achieve your future. For organizations, focusing on the most important outcome means focusing on the customer. *This is STRATEGIC ANSWER #3: the need for every organization to 1) become an outcome-oriented system and 2) focus on the customer.*

This common sense focus on the customer, however, is frequently not the way organizations view their missions. Organizations are often started because either someone invented a better mousetrap (i.e., a product to sell), invested capital (i.e., a profit motive), or secured a government-granted monopoly (i.e., a regulation orientation).

➥ For Example

Compare how your firm is driven vs. these six options by spreading 10 points across all six choices:

_____ (1) Regulatory; the "why"

_____ (2) Operations; the "how"

_____ (3) Profits; the "why"

_____ (4) Products; the "what"

_____ (5) Employees; the "how"

_____ (6) Customers; the "who"

If you selected Option (6) with the highest number of points as to how you are driven, **then see the next list** to verify if you really are driven by the characteristics of a Customer-Focused Organization.

15

➡ For Example

We have copyrighted these characteristics into our **Key Commandments of Customer-Focused Organizations,** based on best-practices research in this area.

Assess how your organization matches up to these characteristics on a scale from 1 (Low)–10 (High):

		Customer-Focused Organizations
_____	1.	They are close to the customer—especially senior executives, who meet and dialogue with them face-to-face on a regular basis out in the marketplace.
_____	2.	Executives include the customers in their decisions, focus groups, meetings, planning, and deliberations.
_____	3.	They know and anticipate the customers' needs, wants, and desires as they change.
_____	4.	Surpassing customer needs is the driving force of the entire organization.
_____	5.	They survey customer satisfaction with their products and services on a regular basis.
_____	6.	They hold a clear position in the marketplace vs. the competition (in the eyes of the customer).
_____	7.	They focus on Creating Customer Value—i.e., "value-added" benefits to the customer through **Quality** products and services, **Customer Choice, Responsiveness**, delivery, speed, **Service** vs. **Total Cost** of doing business.
_____	8.	They set quality customer-service standards—expectations that are specific and measurable to **each department**.
_____	9.	The Customer Service Standards are based on customer input and focus groups.

(continued)

		Customer-Focused Organizations *(concluded)*
_____	10.	They require everyone in the organization to experience **moments of truth** by meeting and serving the customer directly . . . at least one **day every year**.
_____	11.	They focus and reengineer the business processes based on customer needs and perceptions . . . and do it across functions.
_____	12.	They focus the organization structure on the marketplace— i.e., structure the organization by customer markets (1 customer = 1 representative).
_____	13.	They reward customer-focused behaviors (especially cross-functional teams that work together to serve the customer).
_____	14.	They have a clear policy . . . and the heavy use of recovery strategies to surpass customer expectations.
_____	15.	They hire and promote "customer friendly" people.

The focus of this guide is our Customer-Focused, Strategic Management Model, which has just been reinvented, based on:

(1) customer needs and desired outcomes

(2) extensive research in General Systems Theory

(3) the author's professional experience

(4) practical application and refinement

Most importantly, however, is that this model is the result of a comprehensive literature search and a comparative analysis of 14 other popular strategic planning models. ***The most disturbing elements missing from** all *of these 14 models reviewed were a holistic approach and a focus on customer outcomes as the primary purpose of all enterprises.**

THE ORGANIZATION AS A SYSTEM
(from General Systems Theory)

Any organization is a living system—a complex network of inputs, interactions, processes, and outputs from employees, suppliers, and customers. Management and organizations need a set of concepts and tools for wiring, fitting, and aligning these concepts together with some sense of integrity of effort. Any organization will function best when all these interactions, processes, departments, and employees work together in an integrated, collaborative, and cross-functional fashion, supporting the firm's overall Vision, Goals, Outputs, Results, and Purposes. (You pick the term; it does not matter.) It must be used to think, plan, act, and communicate throughout the organization.

The best way to describe any "system" is with a series of Inputs to a Process or Throughput that creates value added, to Outputs into the External Environment that the Customer will buy, use, desire, and appreciate. Those four characteristics, along with a Feedback Loop, comprise some of the main components of General Systems Theory (GST)— the most basic way to look at any living system.

When you use this Framework, it becomes obvious that satisfying your customer's needs and wants should be the *primary purpose or focus* of your organization as a system (versus becoming enslaved by obsolete activities as ends in themselves). This is especially important for Public Sector and Not-For-Profit organizations, who do not have the profit motive to keep them focused on the customer and on outputs.

II. The ABCs of
Strategic Management

The accompanying model and chart shows that Strategic Thinking is composed of four distinct phases (A,B,C,D) and a fifth element, E (the Environment). *We call these the ABCs of Strategic Management.* The reason for this is that any system (and especially an organization) can be described by four main phases (see following figure). This is because systems are made up of a set of components that work together for the overall objective of the whole (output).

➥ Thus

> A system is defined as a series of inputs (Phase C) to a throughput or actions (Phase D) to achieve your outputs (Phase A) within the environment (E), along with a feedback loop (Phase B) to measure success.

Our A-B-C-D-E Phases start with the Future because we want to be proactive in creating our Ideal Future. This way of thinking not only can be used in Strategic and Business Planning (as we shall see in the rest of this Guide), but it is actually a different way of thinking in our lives. It can fundamentally change your life to begin thinking backwards from your Ideal Future (Phase A) on a regular basis. Once you do, then you will manage your life in a more proactive manner the same way the best organizations do.

The Systems Thinking Approach

(Five Key Elements)

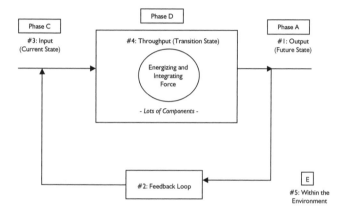

Systems Thinking: Simplicity

A NEW ORIENTATION TO LIFE

(A–E: Five Key Elements)

"From Complexity to Simplicity"

Systems: Systems are made up of a set of components that work together for the overall objective of the whole (output).

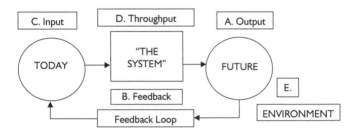

Five Questions in Sequence

A Where do we want to be? (i.e., our ends, outcomes, purposes, goals, holistic vision)

B How will we know when we get there? (i.e., the customers' needs and wants connected into a quantifiable feedback system)

C Where are we now? (i.e., today's issues and problems)

D How do we get there? (i.e., close the gap from C ➔ A in a complete holistic way, ongoing)

E What is likely to change in your environment in the future?

(continued)

21

A–E: Five Key Elements *(concluded)*

Analytic Thinking

1. Starts with today—the current state, issues, and problems.

2. Breaks the issues and/or problems into their smallest components.

3. Addresses each component separately (i.e., maximizes the solution).

4. Has no far-reaching vision or goal (just the absence of the problem).

➡ Note

In systems thinking, the whole is primary and the parts are secondary (not vice-versa).

If you don't know where you're going, any road will get you there.

SEVEN LEVELS OF LIVING SYSTEMS

In addition to the previously stated A-B-C-D Framework and definition of systems, James G. Miller contributed a second key concept about systems that is often overlooked in organizations today. He identified seven levels of systems in his classic book *Living Systems.* These seven different levels of living (or open) systems include:

1. Single cells (as in the cells that make up our physical bodies)

2. Organs (lungs, heart, kidneys, etc.)

3. Organisms (humans, animals, fish, birds, etc.)

4. Groups (teams, departments, strategic business units)

5. Organizations (private, public, not-for-profit)

6. Society (German, French, American, Indonesian, etc.) or Community (defined in various ways)

7. Supranational system (the earth)

These seven levels of different living systems demonstrate that *each system impacts every other system,* and *there is a hierarchy of systems within systems.* What is a system or a department or category to you is only a piece of an organizational system. It also illustrates what is probably the single most important feature of any system: *its performance as a whole is affected by every one of its parts.* When viewed from an organizational perspective, the concept of a systems framework really does constitute a total reinvention of the ways in which we think and do business. It literally creates an environment in which all processes, departments, business units, and subsystems are linked together to achieve the overall organizational system's outcomes (or vision). Later on you will see how, from a practical point of view, we use these seven levels of open systems as a "Cascade of Planning" to tie the entire organization together. One way to view this is in terms of your organization having at least three levels of systems—individual, group (department or business unit), and organization—which require you to "cascade" your planning and change down through each level. It is the only way your strategic management system can continue to move the plan forward and perpetuate its success.

Thus, as you will later see in detail, Strategic Planning and Business Planning are really one in the same process. It is just that the Business Plan must take the Strategic Planning into consideration as a key concept and framework to work within.

In fact, we have already used the Levels of Systems in this Manager's Guide; go back and review the Six Core Competencies of a Leader. They include the systems levels of self/individual, team/organization, and the collision of systems.

The holistic approach we are introducing you to prevents you from making the mistakes so common in other systems.

The 16 Common Mistakes in this reinvented A·B·C·D Strategic and Business Planning Process

1. Failing to integrate planning at all levels (organization-business unit-department-individual).

2. Keeping planning separate from day-to-day management.

3. Conducting long-range forecasting only.

4. Having a scattershot (vs. systems) approach to Strategic and Business Planning.

5. Developing vision, mission, and value statements as just "fluff."

6. Holding yearly weekend retreats as "events."

7. Failing to complete an effective implementation and change process.

8. Violating the "people support what they help create" premise.

9. Conducting business as usual after Strategic Planning (SPOTS Syndrome).

10. Failing to make the tough choices, and resolving conflicts over direction.

11. Lacking a scoreboard; measuring what is easy, not what is important.

12. Failing to define and plan for Strategic Business Units (or Major Program Areas in the Public Sector) and Major Support Departments in an accurate and meaningful way within the overall organization-wide context.

13. Neglecting to use benchmarks to compare yourself with the competition.

14. Seeing the planning document as an end in itself.

15. Having confusing terminology and language.

16. Trying to manage the process yourself instead of relying on professional support.

BENEFITS OF THIS REINVENTED A-B-C-D STRATEGIC MANAGEMENT PROCESS

Now that we have discussed the three goals of strategic management and the three simple elements that form its basis, what are the advantages of implementing our four-phased reinvented strategic and business planning and change processes, based on our Systems Thinking Approach?

1. It is a proactive adaptation to a changing global world and turbulent marketplace. This allows a firm to improve its competitive advantage by conducting a thorough analysis of key success factors, environmental influences, and core strategies.

2. It provides a visionary leadership process, communicating core values and strategies so everyone can align themselves to the same end—**the customer.** This empowers employees, departments, and business units and reduces conflict, thus making decisions easier.

3. It enables the executive team to learn to function as a highly effective team in support of the strategic plan. This modeling of cross-functional teamwork is key to successful implementation. It also enables the executive team for each business unit to do the same.

4. It is also an intense executive/business unit development and strategic orientation process for a new or aspiring executive or union leader.

5. It enables the organization to develop a focused set of strategic, specific, and quantifiable outcome measures of success (including financial, employee, and customer satisfaction). These become the measures of success year after year for the organization as a whole and for the business units.

6. Precise budget cuts during tough economic times can be based on already-agreed-on priorities and goals.

7. It has key stakeholders and business units helping to create the organization's future, rather than being overwhelmed by the uncertainties of change.

8. Executives and employees will be able to make sense out of the confusion resulting from so many different solutions offered by management experts (i.e., TQM, BPR, Service, Teamwork, Alliances, Empowerment).

In summary, another way to view this Strategic Management System of 10 Steps is to think of it as a circle or Yearly Strategic Management System Cycle, which is what it really is. See the illustration on the next page.

YEARLY STRATEGIC MANAGEMENT CYCLE
• Using the Systems Thinking Approach •

Thinking Backwards to the Future

III. Phase A:
Ideal-Future Vision

"Plans are nothing; planning is everything"
—Dwight D. Eisenhower

GOAL #1: Develop Your Strategic or Business Plan
(includes phases A-B-C)

Here are the details of the ABC Phases and Strategic Management
Steps as they relate to Goal #1 of the Strategic Management
System Solution.

Refer to the 10-Step Strategic Management Model on the next
page (especially Step #6) throughout the discussion. In addition,
you can see the 3-Year Business Planning Model on the page
following the 10-Step Model as the one to follow for Business
Planning. Of course, when you compare them both, you'll see
they are basically the same A-B-C-D phases with slightly
different adaptations of Systems Thinking.

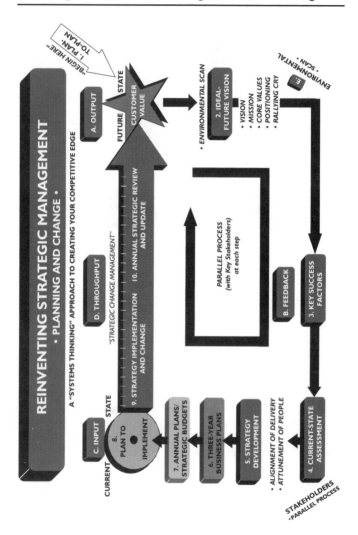

REINVENTING STRATEGIC MANAGEMENT
• PLANNING AND CHANGE •

A "SYSTEMS THINKING" APPROACH TO CREATING YOUR COMPETITIVE EDGE

"BEGIN HERE"
I. PLAN-
TO-PLAN.

A. OUTPUT

FUTURE STATE

CUSTOMER VALUE

• ENVIRONMENTAL SCAN

2. IDEAL-FUTURE VISION
• VISION
• MISSION
• CORE VALUES
• POSITIONING
• RALLYING CRY

E. ENVIRONMENTAL • SCAN •

D. THROUGHPUT

10. ANNUAL STRATEGIC REVIEW AND UPDATE

"STRATEGIC CHANGE MANAGEMENT"

9. STRATEGY IMPLEMENTATION AND CHANGE

PARALLEL PROCESS
(with Key Stakeholders)
at each step

B. FEEDBACK

3. KEY SUCCESS FACTORS

CURRENT STATE

C. INPUT

8. PLAN TO IMPLEMENT

7. ANNUAL PLANS/ STRATEGIC BUDGETS

6. THREE-YEAR BUSINESS PLANS

5. STRATEGY DEVELOPMENT

4. CURRENT-STATE ASSESSMENT

• ALIGNMENT OF DELIVERY
• ATTUNEMENT OF PEOPLE

STAKEHOLDERS
• PARALLEL PROCESS

THREE-YEAR BUSINESS PLANNING

A "SYSTEMS THINKING" APPROACH TO CREATING YOUR COMPETITIVE EDGE

"BEGIN HERE"

1. PLAN-TO-PLAN

A. OUTPUTS

FUTURE STATE

CUSTOMER VALUE

E. ENVIRONMENTAL

A Create Your Own Ideal-Future Vision (within context of Overall Organization's Strategic Plan)
- Duration: 2 days
- Conduct Environmental Scan/Corp. Plan Review
- Refine or develop your vision, mission, and values in draft form (Step #2).
- Develop Key Stakeholder Parallel Process.

D. THROUGHPUT

"STRATEGIC CHANGE MANAGEMENT"

9. STRATEGY IMPLEMENTATION AND CHANGE

10. ANNUAL STRATEGIC REVIEW AND UPDATE

D Strategy Implementation and Change
- Duration: 1 day every 2 months at first
  — finalize Core Strategies/Actions (Steps #5, #6, #7).
  — Conduct Plan-to-Implement (Step #6).
- Set up a quarterly mtg. of the SCLSC (Step #9) to maintain Plan success.

B. FEEDBACK

3. KEY SUCCESS FACTORS

B Feedback Loop
- KSFs not recommended due to time limits
- Instead, monitor Core Strategies, existing financials, and surveys of customers and employees.
- Alternative: use overall KSFs of organization.
- Alternative: add a 3rd day off-site to develop these, and a 1-day follow-up on site.

C. INPUT

CURRENT STATE

8. PLAN TO IMPLEMENT

C Strategy Development
- Duration: 2-3 days, plus 1 day follow-up on site
- Finalize your Ideal-Future Vision (Step #2).
- Conduct Current-State Assessment (Step #4).
- Develop your Core Strategies (Step #5) and 3-Year Action Items (with framework of overall organization's Core Strategies).
- Set up 2nd Key Stakeholder Feedback via the Parallel Process.

PARALLEL PROCESS

31

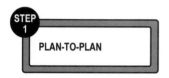

PLAN-TO-PLAN

This step is essential. We will not contract for Strategic or Business Planning before this innovative step is conducted as a one-day "Executive Briefing" for CEOs, Executive Directors, and top executives. This briefing ensures that everyone has a good foundation in the Strategic Planning model, including terminology. The strategic planning process they will tailor together must make sense to the executives and to the consultant. Even if a strategic planning process is not pursued, this briefing and Plan-to-Plan examination is valuable and informative in its own right as a unique diagnostic and learning event.

Strategic issues are identified and discussed in this step, and participants will begin the tasks of environmental scanning and project organizing. This is why we call this step an *"Educating, Organizing, and Tailoring"* day. You will come to understand why you must upgrade your collective leadership skills in order to successfully implement your plans.

The Plan-to-Plan Step usually covers issues such as personal readiness and commitment, barriers to success, planning team membership, staff support roles, and key stakeholder involvement.

Roles of Staff Support and External Consultants

If an organization's strategic or business planning and implementation are to be effective, it is likely to need an external consultant to intelligently facilitate the process and to deal with difficult executive and strategic issues. This person must also work with an internal consultant and a support cadre, who will develop their skills to the point that they can carry on most of the process without the consultant. Until that time, the consultant fulfills the role of a neutral facilitator and devil's advocate, employing the skills of a strategist as well as handling conflict issues that arise in the core planning team's deliberations.

As noted earlier, the resistance to change in humans is substantial; longtime organizational members tend to support the current direction, habits, and status quo. This is true for many senior executives, who have substantial power and authority and the most to lose in change. Our motto in these intense and difficult planning sessions is this: **"If things are going smoothly, we must be doing something wrong."** Executives soon learn in these sessions to disagree without being disagreeable.

Strategic and business planning and the management of change itself are all disciplined, specialized, scientific endeavors in which organizations rarely make a significant internal investment in the necessary knowledge or skills. Business schools and universities have only recently included this subject in their curricula. Thus, most of us have learned about planning and change on-the-job, by observing those who either preserved the status quo, instituted incremental change, or haphazardly coped with "seat of the pants" change.

As a strategist, facilitator, and devil's advocate, the external consultant helps the executives and the core planning team to:

— develop a specific and proven planning process based on the Systems Thinking Approach

— facilitate the planning process without taking over its direction

— stick to their desired values in the planning process

— develop their own concrete decisions, directions, and priorities

— confront the issues whenever backsliding occurs

— keep their focus on Best Practices research

— develop internal consultants/support to take over the process

— and finally, they must be cheerleaders who exemplify and promote a primary faith in people, and their vision and will to achieve.

You will need a lot of support during the full planning and implementation process. Here are some recommendations:

Strategic Planning   Task

Staff Support Team

List names of Staff Support Team:

Position	Typical Tasks	Name
Planning	Strategic/Annual Planning Business Planning Current-State Assessment	
Finance	Key Success Factor Coordinator Budgeting Current-State Assessment	
Human Resources	Performance/rewards management Training and Development	
Communications	Updates after each meeting Print final plan/plaques Rollout Plan	
Administrative Assistant	Logistics/Follow-up Laptop Minutes/Document Revisions Drafts Strategic Plan	
Internal Coordinator coordinates or carries out several tasks themselves	**Minimum List** Parallel Process Internal Facilitator Coordinates entire process Facilitates SCLSC Teaches organization about this	
External Consultant	Facilitates Planning Team Develops Internal Coordinator Devil's Advocate/tough choices Advisor on all planning/change	

TAILORED TO YOUR NEEDS

Finally, after the educational component, the Plan-to-Plan day-long session organizes and tailors the process to your unique needs and to your annual planning and budgeting time frames. It also addresses the importance of having a strategic change management process ready to go when planning is complete. See the chart on the next page for the format/exercise we use to do this.

This last commitment involves the transformation of your business into a Customer-Focused organization via our Three-Part/Three-Goal Strategic Management Systems Solution. It is vital that you are familiar with this BEFORE you begin, because you usually have only one opportunity to do strategic and/or business planning.

In summary, this Plan-to-Plan step and all its tasks (see chart of additional ones) are vital to educate and organize *yourself* before you begin the actual Strategic or Business Planning. You must learn to **clarify and simplify** everything you do when designing and building a customer-focused high-performance organization.

Reinvented Strategic Management   Task

(Tailored to Your Needs)

Based on your current understanding of the Strategic Planning and Change Management models, rate the importance (H-M-L) of developing each potential deliverable for your organization.

Strategic Planning—Steps #2–5

1.	_____	Environmental Scanning (SKEPTIC)
2.	_____	Vision—our ideal future, aspirations, guiding star
3.	_____	Mission—Who, What, Why we exist
4.	_____	Values—our Guiding Principles, to guide organizational behaviors
5.	_____	Driving Force(s)—positioning, our competitive edge
5a.	_____	Rallying Cry—3–6 key motivational words
6.	_____	Key Success Factors—quantifiable measures of success
7.	_____	Current-State Assessment
7a.	_____	Scenario/Contingency Planning
8.	_____	Core Strategies—major means, approaches, methods to achieve our vision
8a.	_____	Actions/Yearly Priorities for each core strategy

Business Units—Step #6

9.	_____	SBU/MPAs defined—Strategic Business Units/market segments, or Major Program Areas

(continued)

Reinvented Strategic Management　　　　Task
(continued)

9a. _____ Business/Key Support Plans—3-year mini strategic plans for units

Annual Plans—Step #7

10. _____ Annual plans/priorities (department plans)

11. _____ Resource Allocation/Strategic Budgeting (including guidelines)

Individuals/Teams

12. _____ Individual Performance Management System—tied to strategic planning

12a. _____ Rewards and Recognition System—tied to strategic planning

Bridge the Gap—Step #8

13. _____ Plan-to-Implement Day—Get educated and organized, and tailor our change management process/structures

Focus on the Vital Few ("STAR" Results)

14a. _____ Quality products and services

14b. _____ Customer Service

14c. _____ Speed/Responsiveness/Convenience for the customer

14d. _____ Choice, Fashion, Control, Customized

Alignment of Delivery—Step #9

15a. _____ Organization Structure/Redesign

15b. _____ Business Process Reengineering—to lower costs/improve response *(customer-focused)*

(continued)

Reinvented Strategic Management   Task
(concluded)

15c.	_____	Blow Out Bureaucracy (and Waste)
15d.	_____	Information Technology—Technology Steering Group

Attunement of People/Support Systems—Step #9

16a.	_____	Professional management and leadership competencies, skills
16b.	_____	Management Change skills/Managing Strategic Change skills
16c.	_____	HR Programs/Processes—Employee Development Board
16d.	_____	Values/Cultural Change skills
16e.	_____	Employee Involvement/Participative Management Skills/Empowerment
16f.	_____	Strategic Communications: knowledge and skills

Yearly Update—Step #10

17.	_____	Annual Strategic Review and Update

Teamwork

18a.	_____	Teamwork for executive team
18b.	_____	Teamwork for department teams
18c.	_____	Teamwork for cross-functional relationships/teams
18d.	_____	Strategic alliances

Plan-to-Plan Tasks

TASK #

1. Organization Specifications sheet

2. A High Performance Organization mini survey

3. Pre-Work Strategic Planning briefing questionnaire

4. Executive Briefing on Strategic Planning

5. Personal Readiness/Experiences in Strategic Planning

6. Strategic Planning Process (past levels of effectiveness)

7. Readiness Steps and Actions (barriers and issues)

8. Organizational Fact Sheet for Strategic Planning

9. Strategic Issues list

10. Strategic Planning "Staff Support Team" needed

11. Planning Team membership selected

12. Identification of Key Stakeholders

13. Key Stakeholder involvement

TASK #

14. Initial Environmental Scanning/Current-State Assessment required (7 minimum areas)

15. Reinvented Strategic Planning for the 21st Century Model (tailored to your needs)

16. Strategic Planning link (to budgets)

17. Organizational and individual leadership (self-change/training needed)

18. Individual commitment must be high

19. Organizational Commitment (strategic implementation and change)

20. Strategic Planning Updates communicated to others

21. Energizers needed (for our meetings)

22. Strategic Planning meeting (process observer for team building)

23. Action Minutes (format to use)

24. Meeting Processing (guide to use)

25. Meeting Closure-Action-Planning checklist (at end of each meeting)

"The only limits, as always, are those of Vision"

Step 2: THIS IDEAL-FUTURE VISION STEP is concerned with formulating dreams that are worth believing in and fighting for. At this stage in beginning the actual Strategic/Business Planning process, the cry of "It cannot be done!" is irrelevant; how to turn it into reality is pursued after the vision is created. **It is about creating your own future!**

Four challenges are met during this step:

Challenge #1. To conduct a visioning process in order to develop a *Shared-Vision Statement* of your dreams, hopes, and desired image of your future.

Challenge #2. To develop a *Mission Statement* describing why your organization exists, what business it is in, and who serves. *Becoming this customer-focused organization begins here with a clear definition of who your customers are.* The upcoming "Mission Development Triangle Exercise" addresses that.

➡ For Example

> The mission of the highly successful Poway Unified School District in California, developed during its Strategic Planning Process, reflects a forward-looking shift from the traditional educational paradigm of "teaching" over to "learning" (from an activity of teaching to an end or output of learning). District leaders are also clear that their students are their "customers."

41

> **We Believe All Students Can Learn. Our Mission Is:**
> To ensure that each student will master the knowledge and
> develop the skills and attitudes essential for success in school
> and society.

Challenge #3. To articulate *Core Values* that guide day-to-day behavior, and collectively help create your desired culture. See later page on the "Organizational Values Exercise."

Challenge #4. To discuss the need for a *Rallying Cry*–a crisp and concise statement (eight words or less) of the entire Strategic or Business Plan, including its commitment to the customer.

➡ *For Example*

An excellent rallying cry used by Ford Motor Company: "Quality is Job #1." To better understand the four challenges of Step #2, consider the following definitions of this **Ideal-Future Step**:

Ideal-Future Step

Definition:

1. **Vision: Aspirational—Idealistic**   *"Our Guiding Star"*
   - Our view/image of what the ideal future looks like at time "X"
   - It has dreamlike qualities, future hopes, and aspirations, even if they are never fully attainable.
   - An energizing, positive, and inspiring statement of where and what we want to be in the future

2. **Mission: Pragmatic—Realistic**   *"Our Unique Purpose"*
   - What business are we in? (not the activities we do)
   - Why we exist—our reason for being (raison d' être)
   - The purpose toward which we commit our work life
   - What we produce—its benefits/outcomes
   - Who we serve—our customers/clients

3. **Core Values: Our Beliefs**   *"What We Believe In"*
   - How do we/should we act while accomplishing this business/mission?
   - The way we do our business—*our process*
   - Principles that guide our daily behaviors
   - What we believe in and how we will act at work

4. **Positioning: Our Driving Force— Distinctiveness**   *"Our Competitive Edge"*
   - Grand strategy–strategy–strategic intent–competitive advantage
   - What positions us uniquely in the marketplace that causes the customer to do business with us—**Customer Value**

5. **Rallying Cry: Our Essence— Motivational Force**   *"Our Memorizable Essence"*
   - The crisp slogan (8 words or less) that is remembered by employees and that is *the essence* of the vision, mission, and core values (i.e., our driving force/positioning upon which all else revolves)
   - It should be a powerful motivational force for our staff, as it is memorable, memorized, believable, repeatable, **and lived on a daily basis across the organization**—everywhere and in every way.

In today's dynamic environment of global competition and rapid technological growth and obsolescence, changing an organization to become "Customer-Focused" is extremely difficult. This is especially true for organizations that have been successful with product-driven or technological orientations, or public institutions that are monopolies or have protective government mandates. Deregulation of all sorts in the 1980s and 1990s forced organizations to become "Customer Focused" in order to survive (as noted on the earlier "Key Commandments" questionnaire). Focusing on your customer and their wants and needs is fast becoming the last true competitive advantage for organizations. Quality products have become the de facto price of admission to enter an industry. **The Customer must now become the focus!**

Mission-Development Triangle Exercise   Task

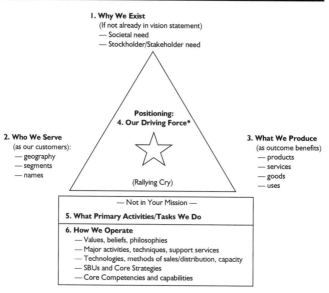

I. Why We Exist
(If not already in vision statement)
— Societal need
— Stockholder/Stakeholder need

Positioning:
4. Our Driving Force*

(Rallying Cry)

2. Who We Serve
(as our customers):
— geography
— segments
— names

3. What We Produce
(as outcome benefits)
— products
— services
— goods
— uses

— Not in Your Mission —

5. What Primary Activities/Tasks We Do

6. How We Operate
— Values, beliefs, philosophies
— Major activities, techniques, support services
— Technologies, methods of sales/distribution, capacity
— SBUs and Core Strategies
— Core Competencies and capabilities

*Note: Your Driving Force can be either a who, a what, a why, or a how (1-2-3-5-6), but it must position you in the marketplace differently from your competitors.

Adapted from: P. Below, G. Morrisey, B. Acomb, *Executive Guide to Strategic Planning,* 1978.

S. Haines, *Internal Sun Co., Inc. Working Paper,* 1979; updated 1996.

J.W. Pfeiffer, L.D. Goodstein, and T. M. Nolan, *Applied Strategic Planning: A How To Do It Guide,* Pfeiffer & Co., San Diego, California, 1986.

Organizational Values Exercise   Task

(Guides to Behavior)

Complete Column #1 (The Way It Should Be). Select 10 of the following values that have the most importance to your organization's future success.

Complete Column #2 (The Way It Is Now) at a later time (or as directed).

Column #1 *The way you think it should be ideally*	Column #2 *The way it is now (can also be ideal)*	
_____	_____	1. Adaptation to Change
_____	_____	2. Long-term strategic perspective/ direction
_____	_____	3. Energizing/visionary leadership
_____	_____	4. Risk-taking
_____	_____	5. Innovation/Creativity
_____	_____	6. Marketplace aggressiveness/competitiveness
_____	_____	7. Teamwork/Collaboration
_____	_____	8. Individual/Team/Organization learning
_____	_____	9. Recognition of achievements
_____	_____	10. Waste elimination/Wise use of resources
_____	_____	11. Profitability/Cost-consciousness
_____	_____	12. Quality products/services
_____	_____	13. Customer Service excellence/focus
_____	_____	14. Speed/Responsiveness

(continued)

Organizational Values Exercise (concluded)   Task

_____	_____	15.	Continuous/Process improvement
_____	_____	16.	Growth/Size of organization/revenue
_____	_____	17.	Contribution to society/community
_____	_____	18.	Safety
_____	_____	19.	Stability/Security
_____	_____	20.	Ethical and legal behavior
_____	_____	21.	High staff productivity/performance
_____	_____	22.	Employee development/growth/self-mastery
_____	_____	23.	Dialogue/Openness and trust
_____	_____	24.	Constructive confrontation/Problem solving
_____	_____	25.	Respect/caring for individuals and relationships
_____	_____	26.	Quality of work life/morale
_____	_____	27.	High staff satisfaction
_____	_____	28.	Employee self-initiative/empowerment
_____	_____	29.	Participative management/decision making
_____	_____	30.	Data-based decisions
_____	_____	31.	Diversity and equality of opportunity
_____	_____	32.	Partnerships/alliances
_____	_____	33.	Excellence in all we do

Senior executives in public and private sectors across North America are in a quandary as to how to find the secret of future success. The proliferation of management writings that followed Tom Peters' *In Search Of Excellence* has only added to this dilemma. Many of these writers promise the ONE Holy Grail that will solve all of management's problems. Even TQM, despite its obvious logical importance, is taking a beating in the literature. So how is one to sort out all of today's ideas and fads? Is it now Business Process Reengineering, or Value Change Management that we need? And not TQM? What about Empowerment? Or Leadership? Or Teamwork? Or Service Management? Or _____? (You fill in the blank.)

> *"In every instance, we found that the best run companies stay as close to their customers as is humanly possible."*
> —Tom Peters, et. al.

Fortunately, there is a way to make sense of all these new ideas and fads, and at the same time create a customer-focused organization. It is obvious to leaders in the smartest companies in North America that the customer is #1, and that all else has to flow from the customer. McDonald's, Nordstroms, and Marriott are just a few customer-focused organizations. However, getting to their level of focus usually requires a J. W. Marriott, a Ray Kroc, or a systems-thinking framework in which to get the entire organization thinking AND acting in support of the customer. Actually, we believe the ideal would be the Systems Thinking Approach *and* Ray Kroc. However, in the absence of a Ray Kroc-type in charge over a long period of time, let us create a customer-focused systems framework.

This systems framework will help us understand, make sense of, and even pull together ideas and people. We believe very strongly that the place to begin using this Systems Thinking Framework is to first truly understand that customers want several things. The Systems Thinking Framework answers the question:

What do customers want, quality *or* low price? The answer is both. In fact, customer wants and needs can be viewed as a combination of five potential results we shall call *World Class Star ★ Results*. Knowing that your customer may really want a mix of these five points gives you a better place to begin to create customer value and position your organization or business unit where the real, true competition is. We use the star to illustrate customer needs.

The illustration that follows should be used as a final check on whether your Vision and Mission are specific and complete regarding who your customers are and what they value.

Creating Customer Value: Positioning

World Class "Star" Results—Your Competitive Edge

Perceived Customer Value $= \dfrac{\text{Outputs}}{\text{Inputs}} =$ Multiple Outcomes

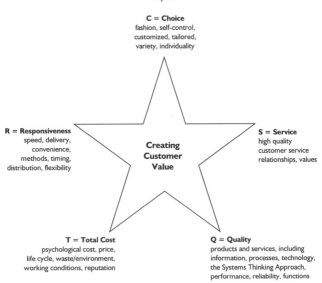

C = Choice
fashion, self-control,
customized, tailored,
variety, individuality

R = Responsiveness
speed, delivery,
convenience,
methods, timing,
distribution, flexibility

Creating Customer Value

S = Service
high quality
customer service
relationships, values

T = Total Cost
psychological cost, price,
life cycle, waste/environment,
working conditions, reputation

Q = Quality
products and services, including
information, processes, technology,
the Systems Thinking Approach,
performance, reliability, functions

Anticipating Customer Wants and Needs
for products, services, and the intangibles

IV. Phase B:
Key Success Factors

Phase B: Quantifiable Outcome Measurements of Success (The Feedback Loop)

"Goal-setting and careful goal selection are the #1 criteria for success."

The second phase of this Model consists of one significant step:

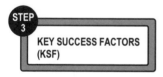

STEP 3

KEY SUCCESS FACTORS (KSF)

This step develops the quantifiable outcome measurements (or Goals) of success in achieving an organization's vision, mission, and core values on a year-by-year basis. This is necessary to ensure continual improvement toward achieving the Ideal-Future Vision. Key Success Factors (KSFs or Goals) lead to concrete answers to three critical questions.

How do you know if you are being successful?
How do you know if you are getting into trouble?
If you are off course, what corrective actions should you take?

First, Key Success Factor (KSF) areas are developed from the key phrases within the Ideal-Future Vision and from key financial and operational results.

Once KSF areas are defined, specific measurements and yearly targets for each KSF area are set. Ten is the maximum preferred number of KSFs, forcing you to focus on what is really "key" to success. Use a Key Success Factors Continuous Improvement Matrix like the one on the next page to plot, track, and report on your success.

Key Success Factors should always measure what is **really important (not just what is easy to measure)** including, as a minimum, (1) customer satisfaction, (2) employee satisfaction, (3) financial viability, and (4) key operational indicators. Others might include product quality, customer service, internal zero defects vs. standards, cost and value, speed, delivery and response time, choice, and customization, as well as being environmentally responsible.

➥ For Example

British Columbia Systems Corporation's Key Success Factors were service value, service quality, employee satisfaction, and financial viability. As an integrated information services firm serving the public sector, these KSFs were crucial to achieve their Vision. Financial viability alone is necessary to that vision, but it is not enough. The organization's failure to understand all their customers' needs led to their downfall.

Note: The Balanced Scorecard, a popular term (and book), identified the same four measurement areas we did. The authors came to the same conclusions that we did years before.

Key Success Factor Continuous Improvement Matrix (Backwards Thinking)

KSF Overall Coordinator for Accountability is _____ (Name/Title)

KSF areas (headers) with specific factors for each	Baseline Target	Intermediate Targets				Target		Ultimate Target	Competitive Benchmark	Key Success Factors Accountability
	1999	2000	2001	2002	2003	2004				
I. Header: Factors:										1.
										2.
2.										3.
3.										4.
4.										5.
5.										

V. Phase C:
From Assessment to Strategy

Phase C: Converting Strategy to Operations (The Input to Act)

"If you don't know where you're going, any road will get you there."

This phase of the 21st Century Strategic and Business Planning Model takes stock of current conditions and establishes core strategies as the organizing framework to guide the rest of the Cascade of Planning—from strategic to operational to the individual levels.

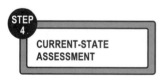

STEP 4.

CURRENT-STATE ASSESSMENT

This step is where internal and external analyses (Strengths, Weaknesses, Opportunities, and Threats—SWOTs) are conducted. Then, the gaps between those analyses and the organization's vision are examined. The Executive Summary of a Current-State Assessment is the actual SWOT technique. (Described later in this chapter.)

In traditional strategic or business planning, this step is the first and main step, leading to long-range planning that merely projects the current state of an organization incrementally into the future.

The good news about the history of strategic and business planning is that there are a large number of tools to use in conducting these analyses. We have developed a list of 10 assessments each organization should do, at the very least (see the next page).

Note: The Current-State Assessment, Step 4, is one place where you can see the difference between strategic planning and business planning. In business planning, an organization *actually competes with other organizations* in products and services for customer and market share. As a result, Step 6 of business planning should definitely include customer-market-products-services and competitor analyses. Samples of the forms we use for assessment are included in this chapter.

➤ *For Example*

> The Palomar-Pomerado Health System in California did a thorough analysis of each major health care system in their marketplace. These analyses were crucial in their deliberations as to how to compete in an industry of shrinking margins, tougher competition, and calls to restructure and reform health care.

The list of assessment methods needs to include a systems way to assess an organization. To this end, we developed an "Organization-as-a-System Model" to address organizational assessment and fit to the overall Vision.

Step #4	Task

Current-State Assessment

(Ten Minimum Current-State Assessment Areas)

Instructions: When you do your Current-State Assessment you must be sure to conduct enough analyses and scanning. The following are recommended minimums. Carry out this task carefully. Make certain that these assessments are conducted as part of strategic planning.

What to Do	Who to prepare it or do it	By when (or at what S.P. mtg./step)
1. SWOT Analysis		
2. Organization-as-a-System Culture Survey		
3. SKEPTIC Environmental Scanning of: — Socio-demographics — "K"ompetition — Economic climate/environmental impact — Political climate — Technology — Industry (competitors) — Customer/clients		
4. SBU/MPA Information — Pro Forma Matrix today — Product/product line (market share and profitability)		
5. Organization financial analysis: — P/L (or budgets) — Balance sheet		

(continued)

57

Current-State Assessment *(concluded)*

What to Do	Who to prepare it or do it	By when (or at what S.P. mtg./step)
6. Core Values Analysis		
7. 36 Key HR processes		

8.   Focus on the Vital Few:
  a. — Value map
      — Market-oriented
      — Customer-focused
  b. Organization design
  c. Business process reengineering
  d. Management/leadership skills		

9. Rewards for total performance		
10. All Key Success Factors (baseline data on KSF Matrix)		

THE "ORGANIZATION-AS-A-SYSTEM" MODEL

In trying to figure out how to make the Systems Model come to life in a more strategic specific and practical fashion, we conducted a comprehensive literature search in the 1990s and identified over thirteen organization models in use today. (Research available upon request.) However, when tested against the Systems Model, **all of them were found lacking; MOST OF THEM FAILED.**

As a result of what we didn't find, we developed the **"Organization-as-a-System Model,"** adopting the best of the literature search, our experiences, General Systems Theory, and even the earlier Haines Associates Model (1979). We also coined a new phrase describing all these other models in use: **"Partial Systems Thinking."** They are an improvement to previous management fads on the one best way, but still not as fully helpful as they could be as assessment and design guides. They have included more of the "building blocks" needed by successful organizations, but not as many as a Systems Model.

This model actually has its building blocks/organizational components embedded into the four main parts of the Systems Thinking Approach. These Four Phases (designated A,B,C,D) are necessary for a complete systems approach to organizational assessment and design.

Phase A: Satisfying the Customer: Every Systems Model must begin with the Outputs specified first. Again, the main Output is satisfying the customer. What is your Vision of this for your organization?

➥ *For Example*

For Giant Industries of Phoenix, a regional energy company we assisted in Strategic Planning, it is **"Unmatched Service in All We Do!"**

Imperial Corporation of America (ICA), a $13 billion nationwide financial services firm, put it this way:

"Always remember: Our business success and profitability depend on serving our customers better than anyone else."

When it comes to *creating customer value,* what we call "Star Results" are really those things customers want: more choice, higher quality, better services, lower price, and more responsiveness.

Phase B: Feedback Loop: Outcome Measures of Success: Accurate and timely feedback on organizational outputs is always vital to continued success—and especially so in today's dynamic, global, competitive environment. **In reactive organizations** feedback is rarely used. In more **responsible yet traditional organizations,** it usually consists of financial and operational activities. Customer satisfaction and even employee satisfaction measures are usually silent. Our Goals or Key Success Factors are quantifiable outcome measurements of success needed to achieve your Vision, Mission, and Core Values.

Phase C: Input (or Guides to Actions): Strategy: The primary input that should guide an organization's actions is its strategic or business plan (and in particular its core strategies). You do not "do" a Vision, you "do" the strategies and supporting actions that are the primary means to achieving your Vision.

However, **reactive organizations rarely do strategic or business planning**. They are usually focused not on the customer but on crises and survival. Budgets are the only way they do planning. **Traditional organizations** usually focus on three-year straight-line financial forecasts or only do separate department or business-unit planning. It is only the **proactive organizations** that are developing a shared and integrated Vision, with core strategies to achieve it.

Organizations can create Customer-Focused organizations without a strategic or business plan to drive the organization forward. However, if strategic or business planning is done correctly, it becomes a tremendous help. **Strategic and business planning should lead the way in developing the core strategies** that lead to much of what passes for major change projects today. With a good strategic plan and core strategies, strategic change projects such as TQM, Service Management, Empowerment, New Product Development, Self-Directed Work Teams, Continuous Improvement, Business Process Reengineering, and the like become much more powerful and central to the entire organization. This is true in both the public and private sectors.

Each of these strategic solutions is correct and effective in its own right. However, when viewed in a systems context, they are only partial solutions and therefore are only partially successful. On the other hand, if they are looked at as a part of the overall strategic plan, then the plan can lead the way to a fully successful implementation.

This is what the Systems Thinking Approach is all about. It is the idea of building an organization in which each piece and partial solution has the fit, alignment, and integrity with your overall organization as a system—and its outcome of serving the customer. See the next page for a list of ways TQM can be the driving force of an organization through integration of its efforts throughout all 4 A-B-C-D phases—"Strategic Planning, Management, and Leadership Leads the Way." It will help you fully appreciate why these strategies are only partial solutions.

Strategic Planning Leads the Way

TQM = Total Quality Management (System)

Strategic Planning is the one major organizational intervention to use if you wish to develop a shared vision of your future and the values, culture, and business strategies needed to get there.

It is a way to:

* Accelerate/advance the changes you want to make

* Tie together and increase the importance of other major changes that should be (but usually aren't) part of corporate strategy, with total buy-in/ownership by the organization.

OUTPUTS: A	Step #1	Vision and Mission
	1.	Who: customer focus
	2.	What: quality, service, response, environmental, cost, profitability
	3.	Why: stockholders, stakeholders, customers, society
	Step #2	**Core Values**
	4.	Self-directed work teams
	5.	Employee empowerment/creativity
	6.	Continuous improvement
	7.	GE's Workout (blowout bureaucracy); reinvent government
	8.	Communications effectiveness; drive out fear
FEEDBACK: B	**Step #3**	**Key Success Factors**
	9.	Benchmarking/measurement systems (world class comparisons)
	10.	Employee and customer satisfaction surveys
	11.	Market research
	12.	Executive compensation and other rewards/practices

(continued)

TQM = Total Quality Management (System) *(concluded)*

INPUTS: C	Step #4	Core Strategies
	13.	TQM/TQL—some of Deming's 14 Points
	14.	Service management/quality service
	15.	Speed and response time
	16.	Business process improvement/reengineering
	17.	Improved sales and market-driven culture
	18.	Cost efficiencies, reductions, and productivity improvements
	19.	De-layering
	20.	People as our competitive business advantage
	21.	Culture change
	22.	Organization structure/design

THROUGHPUTS: D	Steps #6–10	Operational Planning and Implementation
	23.	Annual/operations/tactical planning
	24.	Annual budgeting
	25.	Performance management/evaluation system
	26.	Strategic Change Steering Committee/transition management/Q.M.B.S.-P.A.T.s
	27.	Annual strategic reviews and updates, management meetings

ENVIRONMENT: E		
	28.	What is changing in the Environment? (SKEPTIC)

Phase D: Throughput (or Actions): The Fit of Implementation: This phase is the "guts" of what we think of as an organization. **It includes both a "Content" component (what we do) and a "Process" one (how we do it)** when we are trying to master customer-focused strategic change. There are many different ways to categorize the elements that make up an organization.

However, we have chosen the list on the following page as most representative, based on our literature search of 13 other Organizational Models. **The big dilemma we faced in this literature search was the predominance of Partial rather than holistic systems models** that focused on the customer as the primary outcome. You can argue with our menu. However, if you disagree with it, then come up with your own that makes sense to you. Be sure it is a comprehensive system framework and that it makes sense to your organization as well. You need to have a language and a visual model with which to communicate clearly.

THE ORGANIZATION AS A SYSTEM

CREATING ALIGNMENT AND ATTUNEMENT FOR YOUR COMPETITIVE EDGE

D. THROUGHPUT

A. OUTPUT

C. INPUT

B. FEEDBACK

CUSTOMER VALUE

ANNUAL STRATEGIC REVIEW

VISION AND VALUES ACHIEVED

STRATEGIC CHANGE MANAGEMENT PROCESS

ORGANIZATIONAL DESIGN

TEAMS

TECHNOLOGY TOOLS

PROCESS IMPROVEMENT

ALIGNMENT OF DELIVERY PROCESS

ATTUNEMENT OF PEOPLES HEARTS

EMPLOYEE INVOLVEMENT

RESOURCE ALLOCATION

LEADERSHIP & MANAGEMENT

STRATEGIC COMMUNICATIONS

STRATEGIC HUMAN RESOURCE MANAGEMENT PRACTICES

ORGANIZATIONAL CULTURE = WEB OF RELATIONSHIPS

KEY SUCCESS FACTORS

STRATEGIES

STAKEHOLDERS · PARALLEL PROCESS

ENVIRONMENTAL · SCAN ·

4th Edition · Adapted from General Systems Theory and Haines Associates—
Our experiences, literature searches, and continual client feedback.

Some ways to use the menu:

1. **For example: TQM.** In the **reactive organization,** the squeaky wheel gets the grease in order to keep the complainer pacified. However, at G.E., you must be either first or second in your market or they will not waste their resources on you. Your subsidiary will be considered as a possible spinoff sale. If you cannot satisfy the customer, then you cannot satisfy Jack Welch!

2. **For example: Organization Structure.** Key to any organization is its organizational structure, its job and work-flow design, and its philosophy. Unfortunately, **there is no such thing as a perfect organizational structure**; the strengths and weaknesses of each must be managed, no matter what your structure. In addition, the old struggle between centralized and decentralized structures no longer makes sense. Instead, the **key question is what to keep centralized as you decentralize.** Decentralize all that you possibly can in order to stay close to the customer. Further, the old vertically integrated company of the past (such as an oil company) is no longer the most effective. Having too many different businesses to manage can be disastrous, as Philadelphia-based Sun Co. (Sunoco) can attest. One of GM's biggest problems even today is that it is still about 70% vertically integrated, with tremendous fixed costs and excess capacity. The Japanese, on the other hand, have set up interlocking yet independent companies that partner and work together (called *kieretsus*). Now, even North American companies such as Microsoft and Apple are setting up partnerships. Each is trying to retain its core competencies and get the rest of their needs met through partnerships.

3. **For example**: **Public-Private Partnerships.** You now see these everywhere, as governments and school systems find it impossible to go it alone. The problems are too big and the traditional resources are too small. The hierarchies and bureaucracies of the past are outmoded and too slow to change, cumbersome, and just do not work well anymore.

4. **For example: Teams**. Even Chrysler (now Daimler-Chrysler) has set up Japanese-style "Platform Teams" as the structure and way they do business. It has reduced their new car development time to 18 months from 3–5 years. It not only reduces their time to market, allowing a more responsive customer-focused styling, but improves the quality as well. With marketing, design, manufacturing, and engineering working together as a Platform Team from day one, quality issues are resolved and manufacturing is simplified at the outset. Cost is also reduced significantly due to this improved quality and lowered development time. **Synergy and fit of the other menu items in support of the customer's wants and needs are the result.**

5. **For example: Business Processes.** Business process reengineering entails redoing all the systems and processes of the organization. To the extent that the effort is customer-focused and cross-functionally driven, the different kinds of processes and systems that organizations need in order to function can be radically revised and simplified. These processes might include financial, planning, customer service, management controls, new product development, communications, etc. While all of these processes are important, most critical will be the human resource management systems and processes. They are the way in which you empower employees to create themselves as a competitive

business advantage for the customer. Exxon and IBM have long been known for their excellent people management, although IBM changed things somewhat during their 1990s turnaround. G.E.'s well-known "WorkOut" process was an excellent example of how firms can reduce bureaucracy, waste, and inefficiencies in their processes; much of G.E.'s success and profitability in the mid–1990s was due to this effort. Now GE is involved in a reengineering effort entitled "Six Sigma."

6. **For example: Cross-functional Teams.** Such major efforts are rarely led by a single individual anymore. The essence of the modern organization is cross-departmental or horizontal work teams, such as Chrysler's Platform teams. I helped install a similar self-directed work team-oriented culture at GM's new (at the time) Anti-Lock Brake plant in Dayton, Ohio in the early 1990s. Other examples include project team efforts for major technological changes (Boeing), and cross-functional work teams to reengineer the business processes at G.E. (WorkOut). In all these cases, we are now seeing teamwork transcend the "nice to do" phase of the 1980s to become a core value and business strategy of the 1990s and beyond.

➡ *For Example*

Traditionally, work processes were informal; we are only now acknowledging what the Japanese have been doing for years as part of their Kaizen (or continuous improvement) philosophy. They support the customer's wants and needs through cross-functional teams that continuously improve their processes and organizations.

SUMMARY OF ORGANIZATIONAL CULTURE AND THE ORGANIZATION AS A SYSTEM MODEL

Our menu elements need to fit, align, attune, and be integrated with each other in support of the customer. **Remember: The essence of the Organization-as-a-System is not these elements alone but rather their fit and synergy in one design that supports the whole organization's Vision.** This whole is what we often call an organization's "culture." **This concept of fit, alignment, and attunement helps to explain why culture is so resistant to change.** When we change one aspect of an organization's function, the change often conflicts with and meets resistance from the other elements that are not being changed. **The fit, linkage, and relationships among the elements are the essence of this system framework.** Finding the best answer or technique or process for each element, department, or unit is not paramount; that type of "best" approach suboptimizes the whole. **It is the synergy of each unit and element working together in a coordinated and related fashion that breeds excellence.** In other words:

Excellence is a matter of doing 10,000 little things right across *all* elements of an organization as a system. And, since everything everywhere now affects everything else, the key to success is a disciplined fit of the entire system working together in support of the customer.

Thus, changing over to a customer-focused organization means that, in some fashion, one has to change *all* the elements of the menu. Have you ever heard this? **"When culture and strategy collide, which wins? Why, culture, of course!"** This also explains why most people writing about management focus on more than one aspect of organizational change.

If you are serious about a real cultural (and values) change, you have to attack it directly. Mere gradual change that doesn't upset anyone will never get you there. The radical approach to cultural change requires that you:

1. Attack the change radically, directly, and continually as if you are at war with your senior management's leadership behavior and rewards and recognition processes.

2. Change all the menu elements together so that they fit differently in support of the new culture. Be ruthless about this need for fit and synergy.

3. Assess and be strident about changing as many aspects of your organization as possible to fit these new values (see the following Core Values Assessment and Uses).

In any case, these elements in the menu represent all the parts and building blocks or content of an organization when viewed in system terms. However, there is one more essential element of an Organization-as-a-System that needs to be assessed in order to change to a customer-focused organization: **the change process itself.**

The Change Process (or Mega-Guide): A Strategic Change Management System. This "Macro" Guide **acts as a "governor" for all the other elements.** In order to change an organization and become customer-focused, **you must be a maniac with a mission. Pay attention to the change process and manage it strategically, in addition to handling the day-to-day crises.** Otherwise, all the desired changes and good intentions will lose out to the problems of the day.

Core Values Assessment and Uses   Task

Uses: Throughout the entire organization

The following are typical categories where Core Values should appear and be reinforced within an organization. Where else should they appear and be reinforced?

1. **Strategy**
   - Explicit corporate philosophy/value statement—visuals on walls; in rooms

2. **Operational Tasks**
   - Corporate and product advertising
   - New customers and suppliers vs. current customer and supplier treatment and focus
   - Operational tasks of quality and service

3. **Leadership**
   - Flow of orientation and assimilation
   - Job aids/descriptions
   - New executive start-up
   - To whom and how promotions occur (values, consequences assessed); criteria
   - Executive leadership ("walk the talk"); ethical decisions; how we manage

4. **Resources/Technology/ Communications**
   - Internal communication (newsletters, bulletin boards, etc.)
   - Press releases, external publications
   - Image nationwide (as seen by others)
   - Resource-allocation decisions

5. **Structure**
   - Dealing with difficult times/issues (i.e., layoffs, reorganizations)
   - Organization and job design questions

6. **Processes**
   - Recruiting handbook; selection criteria
   - How applicants are treated (vs. values)
   - How "rewards for performance" operate, especially nonfinancial rewards
   - Role of training; training programs
   - Performance evaluation; appraisal forms (assess values adherence); team rewards
   - Policies and procedures (HR, finance, administrative, etc.); day-to-day decisions

7. **Teams**
   - Cross-departmental events, flows, task forces

8. **Macro**
   - Managing change (according to values)
   - Stakeholder relationships (vs. values)

9. **Feedback**
   - This analysis
   - Employee survey
   - 360° Feedback

(continued)

71

Uses: Throughout the entire organization *(concluded)*

Quick Core Values Assessment (Specify *Why*)

Best 2–3	1–2 Most in Need of Improvement
1.	1.
2.	2.
3.	

In every case where we have installed a Strategic Change Leadership Steering Committee to guide a large-scale change project such as TQM or to implement a strategic or business plan we have developed, implementation was quite successful. In the three cases where the organization's leadership did NOT install this Strategic Change Leadership Steering Committee, implementation floundered. This Steering Committee is absolutely essential to track, monitor, report, and refine the planned changes so they have the desired result. **In customer-focused, high performing organizations, strategic change is proactive and systemwide across all these Design Menu elements. They are phased in over time, based on priorities.** In more traditional organizations, change is dealt with as isolated incidents and projects. In reactive organizations, change is at an "avoid pain only" level, with very little follow-through.

➡ For Example

The City of Saskatoon is a wonderfully "undiscovered" Canadian city of 200,000 people, with a beautiful river valley running along the downtown edge. Once city leaders completed their Strategic Plan, they set up a Corporate Committee that meets quarterly to make certain all desired changes actually take place.

➡ For Example

At Giant Industries, senior executives meet every month with their top 15 managers to discuss Strategic Change Management, so that their changes do *not* take three to five years as predicted. They said they couldn't wait that long!

Finally, if you really want to understand this "Organization-as-a-System" Model, complete the High-Performance Organization Survey (on page 75) to see how you compare to a high-performance organization.

Note: Keep in mind:

> A paradigm shift in one aspect of an organization
> (i.e., mission—strategy—vision—culture)
> causes the need for paradigm shifts
> in every aspect of that organization
> (i.e., staffing—structure—technology—leadership, etc.)
>
> —*if*—
>
> you believe in taking a systems view of organizations.

Once your organizational assessment and SWOT is complete, you are ready for Strategy Development, Step #5.

A High-Performance Organization Survey   Task

Directions: (1) Please circle the # that best describes your organization the way it is today. Then total up the scores at the bottom. Refer to the Organization-as-a-System model for details (on page 76).

(2) Draw a line down the page to connect each circle as you go. The result is probably a zigzag showing where your organization's emphasis has been (high #'s) and not been (low #'s). The extent of your zigzag is the extent of your lack of congruence and fit of these parts of your organization with its outputs.

		Reactive Organization			Responsible Organization			21ˢᵗ Century High-Performance Organization			Comments
		A			**B**			**C**			
A.	**Output**										
	1. Achievement of Results	1	2 3 4	5	6 7	8 9	10				
B.	**Feedback**										
	2. Feedback Loop	1	2 3 4	5	6 7	8 9	10				
A–C.	**Strategic Planning**										
	3. Strategic Planning	1	2 3 4	5	6 7	8 9	10				
D.	**Alignment—Delivery**										
	4A. Operational Tasks (Quality/Service)	1	2 3 4	5	6 7	8 9	10				
	4B. Technology	1	2 3 4	5	6 7	8 9	10				
	4C. Resources	1	2 3 4	5	6 7	8 9	10				
	4D. Organizational Design	1	2 3 4	5	6 7	8 9	10				
	4E. Team Development	1	2 3 4	5	6 7	8 9	10				
	4F. Business Processes	1	2 3 4	5	6 7	8 9	10				
D.	**Attunement—People**										
	5A. Leadership and Management	1	2 3 4	5	6 7	8 9	10				
	5B. Employee Involvement	1	2 3 4	5	6 7	8 9	10				
	5C. Strategic Communications	1	2 3 4	5	6 7	8 9	10				
	5D. Human Resources	1	2 3 4	5	6 7	8 9	10				
	5E. Culture Change	1	2 3 4	5	6 7	8 9	10				
D.	**Strategic Change Mgmt. Process**										
	6. Strategic Change Management	1	2 3 4	5	6 7	8 9	10				
	7. Annual Strategic Review	1	2 3 4	5	6 7	8 9	10				
E.	**Environment**										
	8. Environmental Scanning (SKEPTIC)	1	2 3 4	5	6 7	8 9	10				

Total Score = _____ (170 points possible)
A. High Performing Organization = 110–170 points
B. Responsible Organization = 60–110 points
C. Reactive Organization = 0 to 60 points

A High-Performance Work Organization

The Organization as a System
SUMMARY OF BEST PRACTICES RESEARCH:

A diagnostic tool for understanding and managing accelerated change.

Organization as a System		A. Reactive Organization	B. Industrial Age Responsible Organization (Traditional)	C. Systems Age 21st Century High Performance Organization (Traditional)
A. Output	1. Achievement of Results	Survival Level & Conflict Only	Profitability OK or Within Budget	Customer Value (# Results)
B. Feedback	2. Feedback Loop	Rarely Used (Closed System)	Financial/ Operational Measures Only	KSFs/Annual Strategic Reviews/ Org'n Learning
A–C. Strategic Planning	3. Strategic Planning	Survival/Confusion Day-to-Day	3-Year Forecasts/ Operational Planning	Integrated Strategic Management System
D. Alignment (of delivery processes)	4A. Operational Tasks (Quality/ Service) 4B. Technology 4C. Resources 4D. Organizational Design 4E. Team Development 4F. Business Processes	A. Firefighting/Fix It (Low Quality) B. Out of Date C. Squeaky Wheel D. Fragmented E. Adversarial/ Individual Focus F. Personal Control	A. Maintain Only/ Obsolete Tasks B. Piecemeal Technology C. Incrementalism D. Hierarchy and Bureaucracy E. Functional Teams Only F. Bureaucratic/ Department Controls	A. Reputation for High Quality/ Service B. Technology Fit/ Organization C. Resources Clearly Focused D. Networks/Flat Strategic Alliances E. Cross-Functional Self-Managed F. Customer-Focused (Value Chain)
D. Attunement (of people's hearts and minds)	5A. Leadership & Management 5B. Employee Involvement 5C. Strategic Communications 5D. Human Resources 5E. Culture Change	A. Enforcing Blaming (Incompetence) B. Avoid Blame/ Wait C. Minimal/ Negative D. Poor People-Management E. One Man Rule	A. Directing/ Controlling B. Obedient Doers C. Formal/ Newsletter D. Low Risk E. Command and Control	A. 6 Competencies (All System Levels) B. Empowered C. Strategic/ Positive/Open Book D. Empower Employees to Serve Customer E. Participative Leadership (Facilitate/ Support)
D. Strategic Change Management	6. Strategic Change Management	Avoid Pain Only (No Follow-Through)	Isolated Change Projects	Transformational Change-Proactive
	7. Annual Strategic Review	Not on Radar Screen	Department Goals and Objectives	Strategic Plan— Living and Breathing Updated Document
E. Environment	8. Environmental Scanning	Rarely – Closed system	Today Only	Future/Full SKEPTIC

(Paradigm Shift →)

If you always do what you've always done, you'll always get what you've always gotten.

This step creates the core strategies to bridge the gaps between the Ideal-Future Vision and the Current-State Assessment. It results in the development of three to seven core strategies to be implemented organization-wide. These strategies become the organizing principles and priorities used by everyone as a design framework to set annual organizational, departmental, and individual goals.

Each core strategy needs a set of five to fifteen strategic action items to achieve that strategy over the 3–5 year planning horizon. These become the major activities, organizational priorities, and changes required over time that help build 3-Year Business Unit Plans.

Further, you need to identify the top three to four action priorities for each strategy over the next 12 months. These provide direction for everyone in setting their annual department and individual goals. We call them the "must do" action priorities for the organization or business unit as a whole.

The 1990s have seen a proliferation of new strategies as businesses try to cope with these revolutionary times. They include:

- Flexibly and creatively looking for bargains (Giant Industries of AZ)

- Business process reengineering (General Electric and others)

- Speed of product development (Toyota and Chrysler)

- Horizontal integration of related products and byproducts (AM/PM Mini Marts). Also, ethanol plants in Saskatchewan tie in grain farming, use of mash for cattle, steam generation, and transportation.

- Networks and alliances (Apple/Microsoft or Japanese Kieretsus)

- Value-added consumer bargains (larger packaging at the same price, or Nissan selling its Maxima as a "Luxury Sedan")

- Green-friendly environmentally based processes such as solar heat, recycling, and toxic waste clean-up (a whole new industry)

- Mass customization, where a company like Toyota can deliver the exact car you want with all its features in just two weeks

- Rollups of small companies to create dominance (waste-management—BFI)

- Experiences (Rainforest and Hard Rock Cafes)

- Value chain management through teamwork among customers—manufacturers and suppliers

These new strategies are in addition to the ones that were popular in the 1980s, including:

- TQM

- Customer Service

- Capital Leverage

- Divestitures

- Retrenchments and cost reductions

A similar set of strategies is being implemented in the public sector.

13 Strategies of Entrepreneurial Government

1. Steer, don't row (facilitate vs. do it yourself).

2. Empower communities and customers to solve their own problems, rather than simply provide services.

3. Encourage competition rather than monopolies.

4. Be driven by missions, not rules.

5. Be results-oriented by funding outcomes rather than inputs.

6. Meet the needs of the customer, not the bureaucracy.

7. Concentrate on earning and making money, rather than spending it.

8. Stop subsidizing everyone. Adopt a "user-pay" philosophy and charge user fees.

9. Invest in the prevention of problems, rather than cures for crises.

10. Decentralize authority.

11. Solve problems by influencing market forces, rather than creating public programs.

12. Reduce regulations; cut out bureaucracy and insist on risk taking.

13. Privatization (except for essentials not provided elsewhere).

Adapted from *Reinventing Government: How the Entrepreneurial Spirit Is Transforming the Public Sector,* by David Osborne and Ted Gaebler (Addison-Wesley, 1992), and *Governing,* October 1992 (with a rebuttal by H. George Frederickson).

Beware of those strategies that focus chiefly on ways to cut costs through reorganizations, layoffs, business reengineering, budget cutbacks, etc. ***"Cutting" is definitely necessary, but it is not enough for success. The answers will be found in strategies that*** focus on quality products and services that satisfy the customer—strategies that "build." ***"Cutting and Building" strategies are BOTH needed!*** (See the figure on page 82.)

Lastly, in defining your Core Strategies, we have found it extremely helpful to define how they are changing, in order to make it crystal clear to the organization that the status quo will no longer be tolerated.

You need a simple set of phrases that look like these:

Example: CORE STRATEGIES (From → To)

1. Make TQL happen

    From: Buzzword   To: *Culture*

2. Create a customer-focused organization

    From: Inward focus   To: *Customer* focus

3. Modernize Management Information System

    From: Piecemeal   To: *Systems* Solution

4. Manage the implementation and execution of the Strategic Plan

    From: Strategic Planning   To: *Change Management*

5. Enhance our development and effectiveness as members of the PWC team

    From: People as cost   To: People as *assets*

Now that your Core Strategies are clear, it is time to develop the 10–15 or more action items that will help you to achieve this strategy over the life of the strategic plan. You must develop these and *then* identify your top three action priorities for each Core Strategy for the next 12 months.

These Core Strategies and Yearly Action Priorities become the "glue" and organizing framework for annual plans and strategic budgets. They force the organization to think, plan, and act strategically and systems-wide in terms of strategies, rather than functions and turf battles. You want everyone to work toward the same ends in the next year (the "must do" action priorities and their Core Strategies).

Note: How does this all fit together? Take a look at the **standard format strategy** on the next page.

It is important that this framework be developed. We recommend that you form Strategy Sponsorship Teams for each Core Strategy, comprised of three–six (max.) senior/mid-level executives. They need to volunteer and have a *passion* for each strategy so that you can develop teams of "change agents" who are enthusiastic about sponsoring or championing each Core Strategy. They don't *do* the strategy or priority; they *sponsor* it. Accountability and responsibility roles for each core Strategy Sponsorship Team are identified on the list that follows. A team leader will be needed—definitely one of the senior executives of the organization in order to show the importance of this strategy.

If you do this, you will be developing over 42 leadership advocates for the future (seven strategies with six change agents each) to counteract the pull and resistance of today's organization and the status quo. Without Strategy Sponsorship Teams, the future will lose out to the day-to-day.

TURN-AROUNDS, RENEWALS, AND STRATEGIC PLANNING
(Selecting Your Strategies)

Follow the Rollercoaster of Change Sequence

NEED FOR CHANGE

#1 Today—Cost Cutting—Efficiencies

"Cutting"
(Playing not-to-lose)
Typical Financial Strategies:
1. Cut costs
2. Reorganize
3. Do Business Process Reengineering (Waste)
4. Institute Layoffs/Selloffs
(These are "necessary but not sufficient")

(Turn-arounds)
"Bailing Out"

1. Shock/Denial

2. Depression/Anger

Hang-In
(Persevere)

3. Hope/Adjustments

Two Renewal Strategies:
1. Cost Cutting
2. Building a Future Vision

4. Rebuild

#2 The Future—A Strategic Plan—Effectiveness

(Competitive Advantage)
"Moving Forward"

"Building"
(Playing to win)
Typical Success Strategies:
1. Customer-Focused, Value-Added "Star" Strategies
2. TQM/TQL—Products/Services
3. Service Quality
4. Delivery/Speed/Response
5. And Lots More

VISION

Accountability and Responsibility of Each Core Strategy

Strategy Sponsorship Teams (SSTs)

Roles of these SST champions — to "keep the strategy alive"

1. To be kept informed of the status of the core strategy's actual implementation.

2. To actively support and perform a leadership role in advocating this core strategy across the organization.

3. To cajole/agitate and otherwise push and influence the people who are organizationally responsible to implement this core strategy and keep it moving forward (i.e., reverse the "entropy" that usually occurs with achieving change within a day-to-day context).

4. To advise and recommend actions needed to achieve this core strategy.

5. To actively track and monitor the core strategy's success and report on it at quarterly SCLSC meetings.

(continued)

Strategy Sponsorship Teams (SSTs) *(concluded)*

SST For Each Core Strategy (Sponsors, Leaders, Champions)	Line Manager (Still Accountable for all Core Strategies)
1. Accountable to be "devil's advocate"; to cajole, push, lead, agitate for these to change/succeed.	1. Continue to be accountable/responsible for actions/results.
2. Report quarterly to the SCLSC on the status of the Core Strategy. Use the KISS method—mostly verbal reports/dialogue is desired.	2. Develop annual department plans for your area of responsibility around each Core Strategy in order to support/contribute to, and help achieve each one.
3. Receive all department plans for this Core Strategy. Review/critique them.	3. Track, monitor, correct, and reward achievement of the actions.
4. Support and work with line managers on coordination and achievement of this Core Strategy. Do it in such a way that line manager has no surprises at the quarterly SCLSC meeting.	4. Work with and keep SST informed of actions/priorities of the Annual Plan company-wide.
5. Can increase in size beyond the Strategic Planning Committee membership if needed.	5. Can be a member of SST as well.
	6. Participates in the quarterly SCLSC meeting discussions and future actions.

Possible Secondary Role for SST

6. Can grow beyond SST concept into becoming a proactive coordinator or task force (halfway to becoming accountable).

SST Non-Role (Absolutely)

7. Do not take over the line managers' direct accountability and allow them to assume a passive role. **This is wrong!**

"Systems are sets of components that work together for the overall objective of the whole."

This three-year business planning step answers the question of how core strategies are to be implemented by the different organizational parts. To do this, the business or program units that make up the organization's overall business portfolio (Strategic Business Units or Major Program Areas) must be identified and prioritized based on their importance to the organization's future growth, profitability, and direction. SBUs are developed for any number of reasons. (See the next page for some of these reasons.)

Each Strategic Business Unit/ Major Program Area must develop its own concrete three-year business plan to carry out the core overall strategies. In addition, business plans for the "*major support departments*" (i.e., Human Resources, Marketing, Finance) are also crucial to ensure proper support for these business units.

While we've put 3-Year Business Planning here as Step #6, it is the same A-B-C-D Systems Model for a business unit as it is for the organization as a whole. Step #6 is an *ideal* proper sequence for business units. However, as a practical matter, we often see business planning occur in two ways:

1. Because of the need to do yearly budgeting at a certain time, we often see 3-Year Business Planning delayed for about 3–6 months to finish Step #7 and Step #8 first.

2. We often see 3-Year Business Plans developed first, even before the organization's Strategic Plan. Business unit managers often prefer this; the plan can then be used as the model for the whole organization.

SBUs/MPAs Explained

SBUs, MPAs, Divisions, Units, etc.

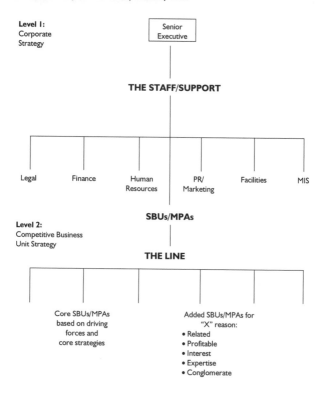

Level 1:
Corporate
Strategy

Senior
Executive

THE STAFF/SUPPORT

Legal	Finance	Human Resources	PR/ Marketing	Facilities	MIS

SBUs/MPAs

Level 2:
Competitive Business
Unit Strategy

THE LINE

Core SBUs/MPAs
based on driving
forces and
core strategies

Added SBUs/MPAs for
"X" reason:
• Related
• Profitable
• Interest
• Expertise
• Conglomerate

The *"Cascade of Planning"* concept illustrates how the corporate strategic plan is brought down level by level so that meaningful work plans can be developed by those who will be using them. *This is the meaning of empowerment:* **strategic consistency, yet operational flexibility!**

➡️ *For Example*

> Giant Industries, a regional energy company, had five different business units conduct three-year Business Plans once their corporate plan was completed. The impact was obvious: 75 (15 × 5) executives and middle managers became fully committed to implementing their strategic and business plans.

This Cascade of Planning is not generally understood, and that's where most organizations go wrong. They draw up department objectives and individual key-results areas instead of *using the Core Strategies as the framework for every department goal and each individual's contribution to the overall Plan.*

This explicit link between levels is the best way we have ever seen to gain everyone's commitment, and we believe it is one of the three things organizations most often do wrong in Implementing Strategic and Business Plans. Specific mechanics of how to do it correctly are covered in Step 7.

Cascade of Planning: Shared Strategies

STRATEGIC CONSISTENCY *AND* OPERATIONAL FLEXIBILITY

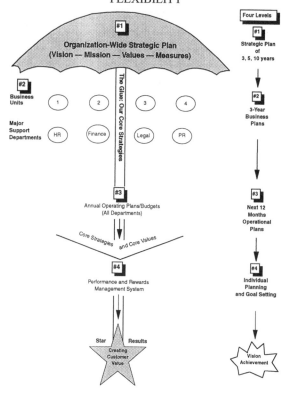

Key: Use the Core Strategies as the "Organization Principles" at all levels

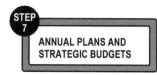

STEP 7

ANNUAL PLANS AND STRATEGIC BUDGETS

Excellence is a matter of doing 10,000 things right.

This is where the rubber meets the road. It is where you develop unit plans with prioritized tasks, and then provide the resources to actually implement your core strategies.

As we said, each department needs to develop a 12-month annual department plan using the format on the next page. The core strategies make up the organizing framework. Use the top three priorities under each core strategy to focus the entire organization; the Annual Plan format will help you do this.

It is not enough, however, to have each unit develop their own isolated annual plans. A Large-Group Review Meeting of the full collective leadership (i.e., top 30–50 people) should be held each year, so that all plans are critiqued and refined based on their fit with annual strategies and priorities.

Then, it is time to change the way budgeting is traditionally done. It needs to be more strategic and follow (not lead) annual planning. This will enable you to achieve a more focused allocation of resources based on the strategic plan and your top three priority must-do's under each core strategy.

The tension between current allocations vs. future priorities is normal and desired. In many cases, internal "Request for Proposal" (RFP) systems are set up to promote immediate projects that move the vision forward. We have provided this list of suggestions for strategic budgeting:

TEN WAYS TO ESTABLISH YOUR BUDGET AND APPROACH TO RESOURCE ALLOCATION

(If money was what it took to be a success, then how did Japan and Germany rise from the ashes?)

Approach #1:	Macro allocations only (let managers decide how things will get done)
Approach #2:	Activity level budgeting (0-based) conducted
Approach #3:	Require 5–10–15% budget-cut projections and plans (cut different amounts, though)
Approach #4:	Budget "hold-backs" (create a pool of funds) for strategic priority uses
Approach #5:	Recommend New Initiative Programs (NIPS) for all funding increases
Note:	You cannot begin the next five approaches at strategic budgeting time. You need to start them earlier in the year, so that their results in cost savings will be evident at budgeting time.
Approach #6:	Work out the bureaucracy/eliminate waste
Approach #7:	Reengineer your economic structure/ process
Approach #8:	Learning as a critical resource/increased skills and motivation
Approach #9:	Recognition and rewards programs
Approach #10:	Fund raising

➥ *For example*

Colorado's Five-Star School District had to cut back on its budget because of a lack of state funding. The Strategic Planning process enabled the Board of Education to use its Key Success Factors and Core Strategies as the criteria for budget cuts. This was the first time the Board was able to prioritize its limited resources based on an articulated vision of the future.

Lastly, this Cascade of Planning must get down to the individual accountability level. Once the Annual Plan and Budget are in place, a minimum of three other crucial management systems must be installed:

#1 A Performance Management System

#2 A Rewards and Recognition System

#3 Performance Appraisals; they must be tied to support:
— your department's Core Strategies (i.e., results)
— your department's Core Values (i.e., behaviors)
— each person's learning and development needs (i.e., career development)

That is, if you are serious about your Strategic Plan.

ANNUAL WORK PLAN FORMAT

Date: _____
Fiscal Year: _____

#1 Strategies/Goals: (What) _____

Yearly Priority #	Strategic Action Items (Action/Objectives/How?)	Support/Resources Needed	Who Responsible?	Who Else to Involve?	When Done?	Optional: How to Measure?	Status

APPLICATIONS

VI. Phase D:
Implementation

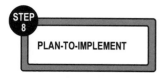

STEP 8

PLAN-TO-IMPLEMENT

"What we think or what we know or what we believe is, in the end, of little consequence. The only thing that matters is what we do."

This step is the bridge between Strategic Planning and strategic change—bridging from Goal #1 (Planning) to Goal #2 (Implementation).

This Plan-to-Implement step is generally done at a one-day off-site event, similar to the Plan-to-Plan step process. The morning is scheduled as an "Educational Briefing" about Strategic Change. It is organized around the Iceberg Theory of Change (see figure on page 95). First, we cover why change efforts fail (see following pages). It might be useful to see where your strengths and weaknesses are in managing change. Note the items that apply to your organization.

A MENU OF CHANGE STRUCTURES NEEDED

First we cover the deepest part of the iceberg, way below the surface of the water—the *structures* needed to manage change effectively. Usually structures are ignored and not set in place, thus causing change efforts to fail before they ever get started.

However, the Primary Change Management Structures are key to beginning change with a high potential of success.

Creating Customer Value

CONTENT—PROCESS—STRUCTURE

THE ICEBERG THEORY AND SYSTEMIC CHANGE
(To Achieve Your Competitive Business Edge)

Efforts:

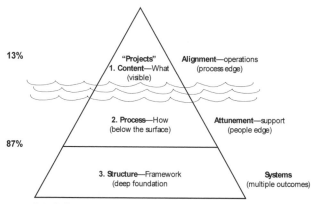

Systemic Change requires a major focus on structure and process,
as well as content, in order to achieve the content/results.

95

WHY CHANGE EFFORTS USUALLY FAIL

> *Most companies don't fail for lack of talent or strategic vision. They fail for lack of execution—the routine "blocking and tackling" that great companies consistently do well and always strive to do better.*
>
> —T.J. Rodgers, *No-Excuses Management*

1. **Underestimate Systems Complexity.** Top-level executives tend to underestimate what it will take. They have unrealistic expectations and fail to understand that the organization is a system of interdependent parts and different levels (individual, team, organization). This results in knee-jerk simple and direct cause-and-effect solutions dealing with symptoms only. Simple solutions for the complexities of interdependent organizations as systems don't work.

2. **Details Lacking.** The failure to specify in sufficient detail the actual work required to implement the change; especially in larger organizations (content/process/structure).

3. **Change Knowledge Missing.** The failure to know, follow, and use what we know about how people deal with change psychologically (the "Rollercoaster of Change." That change has three dimensions—cultural, political, and rational). Discounting the cost of the psychological effects of change or investing in human assets.

4. **Reinforcers Lacking.** The lack of realignment of the business control systems such as performance measures, budgets, MIS, compensation, values. Absence of support and reinforcement/rewards for the new changes.

5. **Accountability Failure.** The lack of specific accountability, responsibility, and consequences at every level of the organization. Inadequate executive accountability and leadership of the change—failure to understand that their role is to actively champion the changes.

6. **Time Pressure.** Too many changes at once and a quick-fix mentality. Too short-term an orientation by the senior executives. Even greed and obsession with short-term, fast-buck, super-profits. Failure to budget adequate "lead" or "lag" time.

7. **Management Resistance.** Middle and first-line management resistance, apathy, or abdication.

8. **Turf Battles.** Opposing and conflicting messages and turf battles in and from top management, along with a split of executive views (as cancer) toward the change. Lack of focused and clear direction, teamwork, and consistency.

9. **Change Structures Missing.** Missing the formal structures, processes, and needed dedicated resources to lead and follow-up on the desired changes.

10. **Reactive Posture.** The failure to act in advance in a proactive fashion; allowing issues to fester and grow, or reacting in a eclectic fashion without a plan or organized framework and philosophy.

11. **Status Quo.** Vested interests and power in the status quo, the auto pilot mind-set/complacency, and the hierarchy can all defeat change efforts.

12. **Stubbornness.** Stupidity and stubbornness by senior management in not using proven research on what works. Instead, relying on their own inadequate models of change, mindlessly imitating the latest fad, or using outmoded theories of motivation.

13. **Control Issues.** Senior executive desire to maintain control over people and events (vs. strategic consistency and operational flexibility) and their low tolerance for uncertainty and ambiguity.

14. **Participative Management Skills Lacking.** Inadequate senior management knowledge and skills on what to do and how to manage change; just plain poor execution—the routine blocking and tackling that great organizations do consistently well. Lack of skills by managers and executives in participative management techniques; including those of trainer, coach, and facilitator. This is where an organization's greatest assets are—with management so they will empower and use employees as their *other* greatest assets.

15. **Fatal Assumption Made.** Making the fatal assumption that everyone is for it and understands it, and that execution is only a matter of following your natural inclinations.

16. **Redistribution Failure.** Failure to redistribute financial resources based on future priorities/direction because strategic budgeting was not done. Denial and unwillingness to make the required tough decisions.

17. **Politically Correct Desire.** The perception that it isn't politically correct to be a strong leader with convictions, expertise, and strong directions/opinions. Putting up with poor performance. It wasn't always like this; megalomania— the one-man show—was once what worked (the benevolent or not-too-benevolent dictator).

18. **Initial Bias Wrong.** A bias toward thinking that success will come if you communicate direction, educate people, form teams, and hold meetings. Bureaucracy and trivial activities will fill up the time allotted.

19. **Lack of Senior Management Modeling.** The unwillingness of senior management to model and gain credibility and trust toward the desired changes first, and to change their leadership and management practices and communications.

20. **Multiple Consultants and Philosophies**. Ineffective use of multiple consultants and/or philosophies on a piecemeal basis. Paradigms and belief in analytic approaches to a systems problem.

21. **Lack of Customer-Focus**. Failure to focus on customer wants and needs and satisfaction as your *only* reason for existence.

22. **Skeptics Not Involved**. Failure to value skeptics and to involve all the necessary people for change. Failing to use high involvement methods, the Parallel Process, and opportunities for personal and group growth and development. People support what they help create!

23. **Poor Cross-Functional Teamwork**. Lack of horizontal, cross-functional communications, teamwork, collaboration, and task forces.

24. **Unsupportive Organizational Design**. Unsupportive organizational structure and design for the desired changes.

25. **Lack of Follow-Through**. The failure to follow-through and sustain the energy, momentum, buy-in and stay-in, effort, and commitment (as well as accountability over the long-term). Perseverance in the face of the first difficulty (vs. pulling the plug) is the key.

26. **Middle Manager Skills Lacking.** Failure to direct, train, empower, leverage, support, and build the skills of middle managers and first-line supervisors.

27. **Poor Communication of Direction.** Insufficient or hazy communication about direction; the single most pressing problem in many organizations.

28. **Cherished Values Violated**. Violation of cherished values without understanding and communicating why and what will replace them.

29. **Debrief and Learn**. Failure to conduct postmortems, debriefs, and distillation of learnings from previous change efforts.

30. **Cultural Diversity**. Failure to understand local, global, cultural, or ethnic diversity—thus taking wrong, insensitive actions.

31. **Lack of a Game Plan.** Failure to have an "Implementation Game Plan" for the process of change—not just the content/tasks of the Strategic Plan.

32. **Political Environment**. The presence of a political and politicized environment, and multiple agendas that block real progress.

33. **Powerlessness**. Inability to make decisions and changes in a timely manner (paralysis/bottlenecking).

WHY CHANGE EFFORTS USUALLY FAIL—SUMMARY

1. Which 3–5 efforts are our change *strengths*? Why?

Strengths?	Why?
1.	
2.	
3.	
4.	
5.	

2. Which 3+ *mistakes* do we usually make?

Mistakes	Why?	Implications
1.		
2.		
3.		
4.		
5.		
6.		
7.		
8.		

Just below the surface of an iceberg—ever persistent but also rarely discussed—is the "process" of organizational change. We call it the *Rollercoaster of Change.*

The Rollercoaster of Change Explained

"Organizational Change" is really a myth. Change is an individual and psychological matter for each of us; the bigger the organization, the more difficult it is to get everyone to change and focus on the customer. *The Rollercoaster of Change* is a term I coined a number of years ago for a phenomenon that occurs and is written about in numerous fields and disciplines, especially mental health. While the terminology may be different, the dynamics are the same and **the *rollercoaster* exists as a reality of life.**

➡ *For Example*

> The question is not "if" each employee will go through the Rollercoaster, but when, how deep, how long will it take, and will they successfully reach the other side. Reaching the other side successfully is quite a challenge for most organizations. Executives were trained in the skill of telling others what to do. In Rollercoaster of Change terms, "telling" is the "skill" of inducing shock and depression in your employees. It is a given that each of us will go through stages #1 and #2 of the Rollercoaster (shock and depression). However, going through stages #3 and #4 (hope and rebuilding) is optional, and depends on someone leading and managing the change process effectively.

Primary Strategic Change Management (Structures and Roles)

"A Menu"

1. **Visionary Leadership**—CEO/Senior Executives with Personal Leadership Plans (PLPs)
   - For repetitive stump speeches and reinforcement
   - To ensure fit/integration of all parts and people toward the same vision/values

2. **Internal Support Cadre** (informal)
   - For day-to-day coordination of implementation process
   - To make certain that the change structures and processes don't lose out day-to-day

3. **Executive Committee**
   - For weekly meetings and attention
   - To ensure follow-up on the top 15–25 priority yearly actions from the Strategic Plan

4. **Strategic Change Leadership Steering Committee** (formal)
   - For bimonthly/quarterly follow-up meetings to track, adjust, and refine everything (including the Vision)
   - To ensure follow-through via a yearly comprehensive map of implementation

*5. **Strategy Sponsorship Teams**
   - For each core strategy and/or major change effort
   - To ensure achievement of each one; including leadership of what needs to change

*6. **Employee Development Board** (Attunement with People's Hearts)
   - For succession—careers—development—core competencies (all levels)—performance management/appraisals
   - To ensure fit with our desired values/culture—and employees as a competitive edge

*7. **Technology Steering Committee/Group**
   - For computer—telecommunications—software fit and integration
   - To ensure "system-wide" fit/coordination around information management

(continued)

"A Menu" *(concluded)*

*8. Strategic Communications System (and Structures)
- For clear two-way dialogue and understanding of the Plan/implementation
- To make certain that everyone is heading in the same direction with the same strategies/values

*9. Measurement and Benchmarking Team
- For collecting and reporting of Key Success Factors, especially customers, employees, competitors
- So there is an outcome/customer focus at all times

10. Annual Department Plans
- For clear and focused department plans that are critiqued, shared, and reviewed
- So there is fit, coordination, and commitment to the core strategies and annual top priorities

11. Whole System Participation
- For input and involvement of all key stakeholders before a decision affecting them is made. Includes Parallel Processes, Search Conferences, management conferences, etc.
- To ensure a critical mass in support of the vision and desired changes

*Subcommittees of #4: the Leadership Steering Committee

How to Manage Large-Scale Organizational Change

1. Clearly define/agree on the new vision.

2. Set up a "Change Management Leadership Steering Committee."

3. Manage the Rollercoaster of Change
    a. *How/where/when* to acknowledge the depression; explain the *why* face-to-face.
    b. How to build in hope and involvement/WIIFM?

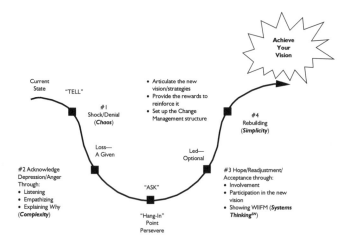

The other catch 22 of the Rollercoaster is the fact that **once you start it, you cannot go back and erase what you started**. Instead, attempting to reverse changes already begun just kicks off another Rollercoaster; this time it will begin where or when you tried to reverse the process. Since this is usually at Stage #2 (depression), it generally means that the new Rollercoaster will take employees deeper down into depression. It will rarely get you out of the hole you are digging for yourself, your firm, and your employees. **What will help people through Stage #2 (depression)? Listening, asking questions, empathizing, constantly explaining the Vision of the Future, and letting people experience first-hand the executive's presence and rationale for the change.**

However, the only way up the right (and optional) side of the Rollercoaster is through leadership and management. In other words, you must be Drucker's "monomaniac with a mission" and have **"persistence, persistence, persistence"** in implementing, correcting, and improving the changes as you go. **Participation and involvement in the change are key to rebuilding the hope of Stage #3.**

In other words, **depression is normal,** and is to be expected as a resistance to change. The worst thing an executive can do is to push people further or tell them they should not feel that way. The more resistance you feel and express to an employee in telling/pushing them, the more they are likely to resist you, as well (the action-reaction syndrome).

This Rollercoaster concept points out how difficult it is to create a critical mass in support of your desired changes. Exhibiting "buy-in" and "stay-in" throughout the Rollercoaster and its bottoming out are both critical. For examples of how this can go wrong, consider the problems former Soviet premier Mikhail Gorbachev had as he tried to reverse his 500-day market economy plan. The ex-communists in the old USSR's People's Congress also had problems trying to reverse Boris Yeltsin's reform programs. Failure to reverse change was the end result of both; chaos was a byproduct.

THE AFTERNOON OF THE PLAN-TO-IMPLEMENT DAY

The afternoon of this Plan-To-Implement Day is taken up with review of our *Year #1 Strategic Change Process Checklist* (see page 109).

It is also a time to organize and establish a "Strategic Change Leadership Steering Committee" (SCLSC) to guide the changes dictated by the strategic plan (see following pages). A roll out and communications plan is created for the newly developed strategic or business planning document. It is finalized during this phase by using the KISS method (10–20 pages in overhead, desktop-publishing format). This allows the planning document to be used in a practical day-to-day fashion vs. the dreaded SPOT Syndrome (Strategic Plan on the Top Shelf, gathering dust).

Step 8 is also when the same 30–50 collective leaders in Step 7 are lined up to participate in a 3-day skill building workshop entitled *"Leading and Mastering Strategic Change." This more-detailed workshop develops and builds the knowledge and skills necessary to manage change successfully.*

Ultimately, a "Yearly Comprehensive Map" of all these implementation processes is developed to summarize your first year's game plan (see page 115). This becomes the final page in the Strategic Planning document.

The afternoon culminates in the presentation of **Personal Leadership Plans** by top management—what they are personally committed to doing and leading (Goal #2—successful implementation).

This afternoon is also when the Strategy Sponsorship Teams are transformed into change agent teams who will track and report on each Core Strategy at each Steering Committee meeting. Usually they are given time to meet and get organized.

➡ For Example

Pacific Gas & Electric's marketing organization planned bimonthly SCLSC meetings in order to jump-start their efforts to meet rapidly changing customer demands.

Tailored to Your Needs (Alternative)   Task

Year #1: Strategic Change Process

A shorter list to tailor for transitional/evolutionary change

Status   *** = Absolutes Prevent Failure and Achieve Success**

H-M-L   **Final Year #1 Task Check:** Score this H-M-L, depending
                        on your needs.

_____ *1. Finalize the Strategic Plan.

_____   2. Develop an initial rollout and communications plan.

_____ *3. Establish an organization-wide annual plan reflecting the
               strategic planning action priorities for the first year for
               each Core Strategy.

_____   4. Align the budget to reflect the strategic planning annual
               priorities (at least 33% effective in the first year—i.e.,
               strategic budgeting).

_____   5. Build all department/division/unit annual plans around the
               organization-wide annual priorities/goals.

_____ *6. Hold a peer review meeting and critique—then finalize.

_____   7. Implement 3-year Business Plans for each strategic business
               unit/master support division/executive via "Mini Strategic
               Plans." (Over the next 12 months?)
               —   to verify, extend, and integrate the organization-wide
                   plan

_____ *8. Set up an ongoing quarterly "Strategic Change Leadership
               Steering Committee" to manage the change process, but start
               it monthly or bimonthly at first.

_____   9. Set up all the rest of the change management structures.

_____ *10. Establish a "Master Work Plan" for Year #1 implementation
               and follow-up ("Yearly Map"). Make sure 3 standard agenda
               items are set up for SCLSC plus all these tasks.

_____ *11. Establish a Key Success Factor monitoring, tracking, and
               reporting system/coordinator.

(continued)

109

Year #1: Strategic Change Process   *(continued)*

_____ *12. Revise the performance management and rewards systems (especially the appraisal) to support the desired vision (i.e., Core Strategies and Core Values as evaluation framework).

_____ 13. Examine your *organizational structure,* as well as staff/succession planning and an Employee Development Board, to support the desired vision.

_____ 14. Implement the desired change(s) in both the headquarter's departments and in units/sites/field locations.

_____ 15. Put in place an Environmental Scanning System (ESS).

_____ *16. Obtain senior management's personal commitment to a set of tasks to implement this Strategic Plan (i.e., Personal Leadership Plans).

_____ *17. Identify Internal Staff Support Team and set up their development so that you build your own internal cadre of expertise and the skills (not just knowledge) to carry out your vision and core values.

_____ 18. Make sure that key cross-department "Strategic Change projects" are set up with clear accountability.

_____ 19. Establish a game plan to ensure that a critical mass in favor of the changes is established (rational—political—cultural).

_____ 20. Set in place strategic sponsorship teams for each Core Strategy.

_____ 21. Allocate resources to fund the change process/internal support cadre.

_____ *22. Put in place two *absolutely key* training and development programs with a top-down ("walk-the-talk") fashion:
_____   (a) Mastering Strategic Change, and
_____   (b) Visionary Leadership Practices and Skills
        (and a Leadership Development System)

_____ *23. Set up the dates/process for the Annual Strategic Review (and update) including the diagnostic assessments and large-group annual plans/review meeting.

(continued)

Year #1: Strategic Change Process   *(concluded)*

_____ 24. Put in place a method to reduce costs, bureaucracy, waste, and obsolete tasks, including business process reengineering.

_____ 25. Set up a specific game plan to become customer-driven; include surveys to create customer value.

_____ 26. Identify why change efforts might fail
  — and determine what to do to prevent this from happening

_____ 27. Establish core values assessment and action plan.

_____ 28. Conduct an Organization Assessment and an Organization Design Study and make recommendations using "The Organization-as-a-System" model.

_____ 29. Complete a Strategic Change impact exercise for each core strategy.

_____ 30. Determine each department head's yearly operational management system and use it to cascade this process further down into the entire organization.

Strategic Change Leadership Steering Committee

Committee Meeting Frequency

1. Phase I: Monthly or bimonthly as the process begins
2. Phase II: Quarterly, once the process is functioning smoothly.

Core Steering Group Roles (in-between Strategic Change meetings)

1. Led by the top leader of the organization (i.e., CEO, superintendent, Executive Director) who coordinates regular weekly/monthly meetings of all the other members.

2. Internal Staff Overall Change Management Coordinator responsibility by a competent and credible senior level executive with the time/energy to coordinate the activities—supported by a competent assistant/secretary support person.

3. An Internal Communications Coordinator to make certain that ongoing communications to all key stakeholders are maintained.

4. A Key Success Factor Coordinator to make certain that measures are tracked/reported regularly.

5. An Internal Staff Facilitator involved and trained to take over some of the duties from the external consultant over time.

6. Strategy Sponsorship Team Leaders who are leaders of the cross-functional teams set up previously for each Core Strategy. If not set up, do so at this time.

7. A secretary/support and administrative person with a computer to take notes and keep minutes.

8. Facilitated by an external master consultant who is skilled in this process and in your content areas of change.

Who	How
1. Board of Directors	
2. Middle Managers	
3. All Employees	
4. External Stakeholders	

Change Steering Committee
(Standard Meeting Agenda)

Note: This interactive strategic planning implementation follow-up day is to include learning, change management, and team building.

1. **Welcome**—Agenda—Logistics—Norms—"Last" To Do List Reviewed
Interactive "change" icebreaker (i.e., change is . . .)
Where in the yearly planning cycle/map are we?

2. **Review Status** of Key Success Factors vs. targets (KSF Coordinator)

3. **Learning Activity**: Conduct communications and interpersonal skills, coaching, presenting, facilitating, team building, or other change management skills needed to have the Committee work effectively— and for the change to succeed.

4. **Review Core Strategies**, strategic change projects, and top priority annual action items (Strategic Sponsorship Teams/presenters—be interactive, questions and answers, etc.)

   • List top 3 successes to celebrate

   • List top 3 issues/concerns and address them

   Note: Rollercoaster of Change—Each topic needs to answer three questions:

   a. Where are we as a team on this Rollercoaster?

   b. Where is the rest of the organization? Differences—Location— Department—Level

   c. What actions are needed to bring us all through these desired changes?

5. **Review of Annual Plan Status** (or business/functional plans)

   • For each department, follow-up results obtained

   • Maintain the organization's "systems fit, alignment, and integrity" with any other major changes.

6. **Changing Priorities? Environmental Changes?** (SKEPTIC?)

   • What are they? What will we do about them?

(continued)

113

Change Steering Committee
(Standard Meeting Agenda)
(concluded)

7. **Deepen Change Management Understanding and Assessment**

   At each meeting, cover one new change management tool and apply it to an issue/strategy:

   - Best Practices List
   - Wheel of Detail
   - Empowerment Criteria
   - Cross-Functional Teams
   - HR Management Practices

   - High-Performance Survey
   - "Change Implications" List
   - Menu on Alignment/Attunement
   - Leadership Development Competencies
   - Positioning/Customer Star Results

8. **Communications to Key Stakeholders**
   (Continue the Parallel Process)

   - In writing and face-to-face
   - Stump speeches
   - Unit/department meetings also (cascade communications)

9. **Next Steps**

   - To-Do List reviewed—assign accountability/timing
   - Next Change Steering meeting—prepare agenda
   - Next year's timetable for annual strategic review/planning and budgeting cycle?

10. **Process—How did it go?**

"Yearly Cycle of the Strategic Management System

(Takes Two Years to Institutionalize)

Date	Task
June—Year #1	1. Begin Strategic Planning (Plan-to-Plan: 1 day)
July–October	2. Do Strategic Planning (5–8 days overall)
November	3. Develop Annual Work Plans/Budgets *
January—Year #2	4. Conduct Large Group Department Plan Review (1 day) *
January	5. Conduct Plan-to-Implement (1 day) *
April	6. Quarterly Steering Committee Review Session —or bimonthly—
July	7. Quarterly Steering Committee Review Session
April—July	8. Develop 3-Year Business Plans * (for Business Units/Major Support Departments)
September	9. Evaluate Plan's Year #1 Success—Rewards based on this
October–December	10. Conduct Annual Strategic Review (and Update: 2–4 days overall) *
January—Year #3	11. Develop Updated Annual Department Work Plans/Budgets
January	12. Conduct Large Group Department Plan Review (1 day)
April	13. Quarterly Steering Committee Review Session —or bimonthly—
July	14. Quarterly Steering Committee Review Session
October–December	15. Institutionalized—Strategic Review/Update Again—*as a way of life*

* These are the steps often missed—resulting in failure to implement your Strategic Plan.

GOAL #2   Phase D: Ensure Successful Implementation

STEP
9

STRATEGY IMPLEMENTATION
AND CHANGE

This step results in transforming the strategic or business plan into thousands of individual plans and efforts, and tying a rewards system to it. The integrity of all the organization parts fitting together in support of the Vision is very difficult to achieve and is a key organization design issue. Human Resource issues and programs are one key. So are your business processes. For instance, your performance appraisal should evaluate everyone on their behaviors vs. the Core Values and their contributions to results vs. the Core Strategies of the Strategic Plan.

Implicit in this step is the understanding that we have to manage change before it manages us (in ways we may not like). *Bimonthly or quarterly meetings of the Strategic Change Leadership Steering Committee (SCLSC) are absolutely essential. No organization we have worked with has successfully implemented their Strategic Planning without an effective Steering Committee.* **There are three agenda items that are mandatory (as a minimum) for each of these SCLSC meetings.** They include:

(1)   continually scanning the changing environment for Strategic/Business Planning implications

(2)   tracking, reporting and problem solving Key Success Factor issues

(3)   status of core strategies and top priority actions

WHAT DO WE MEAN BY "STRATEGIC CHANGE"?
(And how do you actually accomplish it?)

Change surrounds us. In fact, we now say that **the only thing that is constant anymore is change.** Not one of the 29 executives in a recent Banff Center for Management course had ever taken a formal academic course on Change or participated in a five-day skills training program on it! Have you?

So, while change may be all around us, it does not necessarily mean we know how change occurs, or how to lead and manage it successfully. **Many of us have "learned" how to change something by having had it "done to us"** earlier in our careers. So, if we have learned anything from our more autocratic bosses of the past, it probably was the wrong way to do it.

What is strategic change and how does one manage it? First of all, strategic (or large scale) change must flow either from a strategic plan or from a strong thrust (or driving force) led by the CEO/Business Unit Head or Executive Director. Anytime the business top executive is not a "monomaniac with a mission" (as Peter Drucker says) to implement the strategic change, chances are the change will be seen as a side program, and not essential to the business. This is what is happening with TQM in a number of firms today. Top management delegates and then bows out of the process, resulting in failure of the desired change.

➥ For Example

> While Ford has believed in "Quality is Job One" for at least a decade and a half (and backed it up with training and a focus on quality), GM has done the opposite. They have a "Quality Network" set up jointly with the UAW, but only give it lip service.

My observations have led me to the conclusion that people at GM did not view the program as a core business strategy (or driving force), and this is why it is not working at GM.

In order to synthesize all the many tasks needed for systemic change into a useful listing, we have compiled a list of ten "Areas" to focus upon for effective Strategic Change.

SO, IF THIS IS STRATEGIC CHANGE, HOW DO I MASTER IT?

If you look at all that's required to create a customer-focused, high-performance organization, it should be obvious that change takes 3–5 years, even with concentrated and continual action. The issues in Mastering Strategic Change are many:

1. The need for a CEO who totally commits to the change effort.

2. The need for a Strategic and Business Plan, and Core Strategies to guide the change.

3. The need to position the organization to navigate the dynamic and global marketplace in which we now exist.

4. The need to truly understand the customer's wants and needs better than our competition does.

5. The need to understand and master the skills embedded in the Rollercoaster of Change (and all its nuances).

6. The ability to create the amount of active support needed to effect the desired changes. Remember: "People support what they help create."

7. The need for people with leadership and management skills who can make sure changes are made successfully, while still paying attention to day-to-day crises (i.e., a Leadership Development System).

8. Installing Strategic Human Resource Management practices to make certain that people are part of your competitive edge.

9. A complete revamping of your Organization Design to fit with the core values and core strategies.

10. And lastly, the need to understand the concept and framework of an Organization-as-a-System to ensure the fit, alignment, attunement, and integrity of all the elements in support of becoming a customer-focused, high-performance organization and creating customer value.

Traditional, analytical, or partial systems thinking will help you focus on those elements of an organization that are important to you personally or professionally. However, you are not likely to be able to pay attention to ALL the needed elements or tracks of an organization.

If the best writers and management theorists of our time don't pay attention to all the elements, why do you think that you will pay attention to them all?

If these 10 issues are key to becoming a customer-focused, high-performance organization, then the next question you must answer is: At what level of Mastery am I now in my SKILLS of managing strategic change?

It is generally assumed that **there are four potential skill levels of professionalism:**

> **#1 Trainee/Rookie**
>
> **#2 Technique-driven**
>
> **#3 Model (or theory)-driven**
>
> **#4 Mastery (or Jazz/strategic) level**

It is commonly accepted that all disciplines or fields of endeavor have these four levels. You may have something in common with the Banff course executives noted earlier who did not have much formal background in managing strategic change. Executives with the skills necessary for changing to or creating a customer-focused organization are even harder to find. A customer-focused organization with a quantifiable measurement system based on a Systems Thinking Framework is definitely NOT the norm for western business and society—and not familiar to most management writers.

Thus, many readers are probably somewhere at the second skill level—that is, utilizing some comfortable techniques. Are those techniques effective, and do they result in the desired changes WITHOUT any unintended negative side effects in the organization?

Unfortunately, the Change Mastery challenge facing most executives is multifaceted:

#1. You must search out and eliminate any change techniques that have unintended negative consequences.

#2. You must as leader master all five steps in the Rollercoaster of Change; not just the skill of telling (or inducing shock and depression).

#3. You have to learn how to use the Organization-as-a-System framework in all that you do, so it becomes second nature in how you think, act, and lead.

#4. You must also develop an "automatic pilot" mentality that keeps EVERYTHING that you and others do focused on the customer. **Remember: the customer is the only reason for your existence.**

#5. Lastly, you will also need to develop the new skills of effective management and leadership: **Trainer, Coach, and Facilitator** (again, your needed leadership development system).

Developing your thinking, management, and leadership skills in the five areas above will certainly bring your skills up to the third skill level of professionalism (a Systems Framework/ Theory). It will result in a marked improvement in your ability to create a highly effective customer-focused organization. However, that still leaves the fourth level of Mastery for those who are responsible for or desire to strategically and successfully lead a large organization of any type—public or private.

This fourth Level is the true Mastery level of Strategic Change, one where you can be a jazz musician. You need that jazz ability to lead your organization in strategic and successful efforts to satisfy (or even exceed) customer wants and business needs. This Mastery Level includes your ability to be flexible yet authentic with your own personal style and the circumstances you are dealing with, and still hold true to your Vision, Strategies, and the customer. You are able to move off the melody, so to speak, the way a great jazz musician can, and still return to the Vision and Framework; you can be faithful to the customer's wants and needs, without missing a beat!

➥ *For Example*

The leader-jazz musician is happy to make exceptions to policies and reacts positively to the innovations and creative ideas that normally make other executives uncomfortable. This kind of leader also encourages changes in any one of the change menu elements that will break with the status quo. Their only question is whether any of this creativity and innovation will *improve* the way they satisfy the customer. Flexibility, encouragement, and positive reaction to creativity and innovation are what allow employees the freedom to act, be empowered, take risks, and not be penalized for it. It is a key skill for today's executives to master, and it is what the Deming "Drive out Fear" principle is all about in TQM.

This executive-level Mastery results in exceeding customer expectations, the only way to retain customer loyalty long-term. Statistics have consistently shown that it is about 5 times as hard (and expensive) to find a new customer as it is to retain a current one.

➡ For Example

On a recent Friday, my travel agency realized it had forgotten to deliver my airplane tickets for a two-week business trip. I was scheduled to leave the next day and travel all across North America. You can imagine the problems (and cost) this forgetfulness created! Not only did I hear from the travel agent, but the owner went out of his way to call and try to help. They never denied the problem; instead, they sent me an apology card at my hotel in a foreign city. They called to again apologize, sent champagne to my hotel room, and said they wanted to pay for any and all added costs I had incurred. They even gave me credits for future travel. *This* is what is meant by Recovery Strategy and Unsurpassed Customer Service with your customers. Forget the policies and costs; just improvise, play jazz, and exceed the customer's expectations when you are recovering from a mistake.

Following-up, correcting mistakes, and showing disciplined persistence and integrity are key in Step #9.

In addition, Step #10 includes an Annual Strategic Review and Update of the Strategic Plan (the key to sustaining your vision over the long-term).

GOAL #3   Sustaining High Performance

STEP 10

ANNUAL STRATEGIC REVIEW (AND UPDATE)

This step is *similar to a yearly independent financial audit* and includes:

(1) Reacting to changes in the environment

(2) Reviewing the Strategic/Business Planning and updating annual action and budgeting priorities for the next 12 months

(3) Updating the Strategic Management System itself, the Strategic Change Leadership Steering Committee, and the Strategy Sponsorship Teams

(4) Reviewing and problem solving the status of the vital-few strategic change leverage points, especially Creating Customer Value

The key to sustaining a customer-focused, high-performance learning organization over the long-term is this formal yearly review (and update). And it is the one step most often overlooked by executives.

The specific Annual Strategic Review and Update process includes five steps:

(1) Contract for a Plan-to-Review by an outside consultant/ impartial observer.

(2) Conduct a strategic review and diagnosis (statistics, interviews, and observations).

(3) Synthesize data, write the report, and make recommendations for improvement.

(4) Hold two Strategic Change Leadership Steering Committee meetings, each two days in length.

Standard Agenda for This First Meeting:

- Receive the report and feedback.
- Discuss its recommendations.
- Update your Strategic Plan—especially re-confirm and/or refine your Vision, Mission, Values, Success Measures, and Core Strategies.
- Conduct an environmental scan and Current-State Assessment (SWOT analysis).
- Make decisions regarding next steps, focusing on the vital few leverage points for strategic change and Customer Value Star Results.
- Set new action plans and priorities for each core strategy to guide this next year's annual planning and budgeting process.
- Make decisions regarding future strategic process and structural mechanisms to guide next year's change process, while building next year's *Yearly Comprehensive Map* of Implementation.

(5) After this off-site meeting, integrate changes into the: (1) quarterly Strategic Change Leadership Steering Committee meetings (2) specific strategic change projects (3) day-to-day tasks, and (4) weekly executive team staff meetings in order to ensure sustained achievement of the Vision over time.

APPLICATIONS

VII. How to Get Started in Strategic Management

OPTION A—Plan-to-Plan: There are *three main ways to get started* with creating your customer-focused organization. The first method is a *one-day Executive Briefing and Plan-to-Plan event (Step #1).* This is an inexpensive way to educate, organize, and create that pursues four objectives:

1. To gain a common set of principles and knowledge about how to reinvent Strategic/Business Planning for the 21st century.

2. To understand that **reinventing Strategic/Business Planning is really a three-part Strategic Management System,** and what that means in terms of our Three Goals toward Creating a Customer-Focused, High-Performance Organization.

3. To diagnose your strategic issues and to examine certain components of your current Strategic/Business Plans as a way to tailor your strategic/business planning and strategic management process.

4. To conduct an actual "Plan-to-Plan" session in order to determine next steps (if any) for a tailored and crafted strategic planning process that fits your unique situation and needs.

OPTION B—Plan-to-Implement: The second way to get started is the *one-day Plan-to-Implement Day (Step #8).* Afterwards, you will be more organized for implementation and change. During the first year of implementation, the Strategic Change Leadership Steering Committee takes the lead in identifying and completing those aspects of the full Strategic Planning process that make sense to them.

OPTION C—Tailored to your needs: Begin anywhere you want on our 10-step strategic planning and strategic management process and then continue on from there— filling in the blanks as you go. For example:

Since we use the Systems Thinking Approach and framework, we can jump in at any point where you need assistance. For example, we can help you:

1. Set up a Strategic Change Leadership Steering Committee to guide and coordinate existing (in process) change.

2. Conduct annual planning via core strategy/goals and yearly action priorities.

3. Finish budgeting and then set up Strategic Change Project Teams for big, cross-functional issues.

4. Have internal staff get trained and licensed to facilitate strategic/business planning.

5. Have internal staff get trained and licensed for Mastering Strategic Change.

6. Conduct a Visionary Leadership Practices Workshop to kick-start strategic/business planning.

7. Conduct a Mastering Strategic Change Workshop simulation to kick-start or re-energize a major change project.

8. Conduct pilot strategic planning for a major support department or a Strategic Business Unit. Use it to learn and to develop internal support.

9. Conduct only the strategic/business planning phase you need now—such as Visioning, measurements (Key Success Factors), or Core Strategy (issues) development . . . and then appoint a Strategic Change Leadership Steering Committee to guide implementation.

10. Arrange to have your management staff trained in strategic planning concepts through a three-day workshop we call *Reinvented Strategic/Business Planning for the 21st Century.*

11. Arrange for a keynote address at your management conference on Strategic Planning/Strategic Change, a one- to two-hour session, using four-color models and summary articles as handouts.

12. Schedule an Annual Strategic Review and Update as a starting point. Then proceed according to the recommendations/decisions from this audit.

This is a long-term process. Quick fixes are not lasting. The Systems Thinking Approach is a multi-year change effort to create customer value and achieve your ideal-future vision.

FINAL SUMMARY

As a final summary, here are the **15 Absolutes for Strategic Management Implementation Success.**

THE TOOLS—TIPS—TECHNIQUES FOR SUCCESSFUL IMPLEMENTATION

1. **Have a clear vision** of your Ideal future, with values and customer-focused outcomes/measures.

2. **Develop focused core strategies;** they are the glue for setting and reviewing annual goals and action plans for all major departments or business units.

3. **Set up Strategic Sponsorship Teams** of cross-functional leaders to develop, track, and monitor each core strategy.

4. **Focus on and phase in the Vital Few Leverage Points** for strategic change over the next 2–5 years, starting immediately with leadership skills—and then focus on being a "Star" in value-added delivery (organization design).

5. **Create a critical mass for change** that goes all out to become self-sustaining, and develops 3-year business plans for all major divisions/departments.

6. **Develop and gain public commitments to the development of personal leadership plans** by all top management leaders—then communicate, communicate, communicate.

7. **Set up an internal cadre—a support team** for overall change-management coordination that reports directly to the CEO/Executive Director.

8. **Establish a Strategic Change Leadership Steering Committee** (led by the CEO, and armed with a yearly Process Map) that meets on a regular basis to guide, lead, and manage all major changes.

9. **Redo your HR management systems** to support the new vision/values, especially your performance/rewards system and your performance appraisal form (evaluate against core values and core strategies).

10. **Institutionalize the parallel process** with all key stakeholders as the new participative way you plan, change, and run your business day-to-day.

11. **Set up KSFs and a tracking system** to ensure clarity/focus on the scoreboard for success.

12. **Use a consistent annual planning format** to link strategies/priorities to annual plans and results.

13. **Set annual priorities** and confine them to two pages to focus everyone on what's important next year.

14. **Conduct annual large-group review meetings** each year so that everyone is up to speed and in sync with everyone else.

15. **Conduct the annual Strategic Review (and Update)** as if it is an independent financial audit, to keep your Strategic Plan updated as a living document.

As you begin to turn your firm into a Customer-Focused, High-Performance Learning Organization, try to follow all the recommendations in this Manager's Guide. However, **it is very difficult to stay focused on the Vital Few Leverage Points for change when you must also take care of trivial daily tasks.** If you are to be successful in your efforts, however, you must be consistent in your *actions.* As Ed Lawlor states in his book *The Ultimate Advantage: Creating the High Involvement Organization:*

> "Sometimes having a good management system is confused with having high-quality employees. This is a mistake—the two are quite different in some important ways: Having high-quality employees does not assure an organization of having a sustainable competitive advantage."

Thus, our final argument in this Guide is this: Today's executives desiring to develop high-performing, customer-focused organizations **need to install a "Strategic Management System" as a new way to run their business day-to-day.** Senior management traditionally spent only 5–10 % of their time on strategic issues.

However, it's no longer adequate; senior management must now spend at least 20% of their time on strategy and strategic thinking . . . and then use that to **STRATEGICALLY MANAGE the organization as an entire SYSTEM (i.e., a Strategic Management System).**

This is what the Centre for Strategic Management does. **We help visionary senior executives and top management teams develop and institutionalize this kind of a system.**

The Strategic Management System is how we assist these executives in the creation of customer-focused, high-performance learning organizations. The processes we have developed and fine-tuned over the years will help align organizations and their people in delivering real value to their customers.

To do this, we place a special emphasis on choosing successful strategies and then focusing on selected areas where we can create customer value and reach optimal performance.

The "art" of creating and managing strategic change is to find a way to balance the processes required to achieve this with the right strategies and content.

Ultimately, Senior Management must show strong leadership, and the organization's Human Resource programs and practices must fit and be integrated to the organization's vision. Again, the key to this is to focus on the five Star Results customers desire . . . and then to work backwards through the organization to deliver on these customer wants and needs—the first time and every time!

Successful navigation of the turbulent waters in today's highly competitive and global marketplace demands a holistic approach that works. If you spend the time planning the right strategy, implementation and sustainment will be successful, as well.

In summary, this Manager's Pocket Guide is your guide toward defining and implementing the actions that come with sound strategic management. It will not always be a smooth path, but to avoid tough choices is to let the future health and performance of your organization be determined by circumstances that are increasingly beyond your control. The proven best-practices and systems approach we recommend will help you successfully design, build, and sustain your Ideal-Future Vision as a customer-focused, high-performance learning organization.

Are you ready to develop the disciplined Systems Thinking Approach needed to create a customer-focused, high-performance organization or business unit?

> *"What we think, or what we know, or what we believe is, in the end, of little consequence . . .*
>
> *The only consequence . . . is what we do!"*

Good Luck in developing your Strategic Management System.

CONCLUSION

VIII. Summary:
Recap of Key Points and Checklists

REINVENTING STRATEGIC AND BUSINESS PLANNING

RECAP OF KEY POINTS

- Look at your organization as having at least three levels—individual, group, and organization. You will need to cascade your planning and change management down to all levels.

- Strategic and business planning should be at the top of your priority list as you integrate new organizational-change concepts like TQM, business process reengineering, empowerment, and customer service.

- Which of the 15 Strategic Management mistakes have you made?

    1. Failing to integrate planning at all levels.
    2. Keeping planning separate from day-to-day management.
    3. Conducting long-range forecasting only.
    4. Taking a random approach to planning.
    5. Developing vision, mission, and value statements that are little more than fluff.

(continued)

REINVENTING STRATEGIC AND BUSINESS PLANNING

RECAP OF KEY POINTS *(continued)*

6. Having yearly weekend retreats as your only planning activity.

7. Failing to complete an effective implementation process.

8. Violating the "people support what they help create" principle.

9. Conducting business-as-usual after strategic planning.

10. Failing to make the tough choices.

11. Failing to keep a scoreboard; measuring what's easy, rather than what's important.

12. Failing to define Strategic Business Units in a meaningful way.

13. Neglecting to compare yourself with the competition.

14. Seeing the planning document as an end in itself.

15. Having confusing terminology and language.

• Which of these are still missing in *your* organization?

1. Taking an organization-wide, proactive approach to a changing global world.

2. Building an executive team that serves as a model of cross-functional or horizontal teamwork.

3. Having an intense executive-development and orientation process.

4. Defining focused, quantifiable-outcome measures of success.

5. Making intelligent budgeting decisions.

(continued)

REINVENTING STRATEGIC AND BUSINESS PLANNING

RECAP OF KEY POINTS *(concluded)*

6. Clarifying your competitive advantage.

7. Reducing conflict; empowering the organization.

8. Providing clear guidelines for day-to-day decision making.

9. Creating a critical mass of support for change.

10. "Singing from the same hymnal" in all of your communications.

11. Clarifying and simplifying the broad range of management techniques.

12. Empowering middle managers.

13. Focusing everyone in the organization on the same overall priorities.

14. Speeding up implementation of your core strategies.

15. Providing tangible tools for dealing with the stress of change.

PLAN-TO-PLAN (STEP #1)

RECAP OF KEY POINTS

- Before you begin the Plan-to-Plan step, make sure you are clear on what it is; i.e., an executive briefing can also be an opportunity to organize your approach to the strategic planning process (educate and organize).

- Be specific and clear on the exact entity you're going to plan for (organization, geographic community sector, business unit, etc.).

- Identify the key issues upfront that are critical to your organization's success, as a guide to keeping planning practical. (Use the strategic/organizational assessment to accomplish this.)

- Make sure the top members of your collective leadership are personally ready and committed to leading your strategic planning and change-management process. (In other words, conduct capacity-building through team-building/visionary leadership priorities and skills training, right away.)

- Use Plan-to-Plan as an opportunity to problem-solve potential barriers to strategic/business planning your organization may encounter—before you begin.

- Be sure to scan your organization's environment, both internal and external, to make certain you're not trying to create your plan in a vacuum. (SKEPTIC)

- Don't blindly follow the ten steps of the planning model . . . tailor your strategic plan in a way that best fits your particular organization.

- Make sure your strategic/business plan drives your budget (i.e., strategic budgeting), not vice versa. Be sure to sequence them over your yearly cycle.

(continued)

PLAN-TO-PLAN (STEP #1)

RECAP OF KEY POINTS *(concluded)*

- Your key stakeholders should include anyone who affects or is affected by the organization's strategic plan.

- Don't let your planning team grow beyond 14 or 15 individuals.

- Create a staff support cadre to support the planning team.

- Have an experienced strategic/business planning facilitator who can play devil's advocate and deal with strong egos.

- Incorporate a parallel process to integrate the planning team's progress with other key stakeholders, inside and outside of the organization. (Communicate . . . communicate . . . communicate!)

- Set up clear, mutually agreed-upon ground rules that will be in effect for the entire planning and implementation process.

- Review and reaffirm all commitments to your organization's plan and the planning process—including the three goals.

- Take 3–5 minutes at the end of each planning day to give yourselves feedback, and try to learn from your experiences. Ask these key questions:

  1. What can we continue to do?

  2. What can we do more of?

  3. What should we do less of?

PLAN-TO-PLAN TASKS

ACTION CHECKLIST

I. Look before you leap. Hold at least a half-day Executive Briefing, in which all top management executives—including the CEO—learn about and get involved with the planning process. Consider including key stakeholders, as well.

II. Hold a kick-off meeting to share information about the planning process with all key stakeholders, and discuss their roles.

III. Select an external strategic/business planning facilitator to start the planning process, but also set up the staff support cadre right away, so you can eventually have the internal capacity to run this process yourself.

IV. Complete all the Plan-to-Plan tasks, either in a formal, half-day session following the executive briefing session or informally with the CEO and top management team. Use this list of 25 tasks as your checklist:

1. Organization-specifications sheet
2. A high-performance organization mini-survey
3. Pre-work strategic-planning briefing questionnaire
4. Executive briefing on strategic management
5. Personal readiness for strategic management
6. Strategic-planning problems/barriers
7. Readiness actions and steps
8. Organizational fact sheet for strategic planning
9. Strategic issues list

(continued)

PLAN-TO-PLAN TASKS

ACTION CHECKLIST *(concluded)*

10. Strategic planning staff-support team/needed meetings
11. Planning-team membership
12. Identification of key stakeholders
13. Key stakeholder involvement
14. Initial environmental scanning/current-state assessment required (7 minimum areas)
15. Reinvented Strategic Planning Model tailored to your needs
16. Strategic planning link to budgets
17. Organizational and individual leadership (self-change)
18. Individual commitment
19. Strategic implementation and change commitments
20. Strategic planning updates communicated to others
21. Energizers for meetings
22. Strategic planning meeting process observer
23. Action minutes format
24. Meeting processing guide
25. Closure/action planning

IDEAL-FUTURE VISION (STEP #2)

RECAP OF KEY POINTS

- The Ideal-Future Vision step is the first real action step in strategic planning . . . and one of the recurring key elements for success.

- The first challenge in the Ideal-Future Vision step is to shape an organizational vision statement.

- The second challenge is to develop a realistic mission statement that describes your organization's desired, unique purpose.

- The third challenge is to develop core values that make up your organization's culture: "What we believe in."

- Challenge #4 is to design a rallying cry or driving force that states the essence of your organization—it's reason for being. It is often better to wait until the end of strategic planning, in order to really clarify the essence of your strategic plan.

- It will be necessary to identify and assess the levels of risk inherent in these challenges.

- Developing a mission can be quite confusing.
    1. You might think the "how" is part of the mission. (It is not.)
    2. You might fail to focus on the customer.
    3. Lack of clarity on "control" vs. "service" in departmental mission statements might not adequately address "control" vs. "service."
    4. You might fail to properly define your "entity" in the public sector.
    5. You might just be going through the motions.

- In developing your vision and mission statements, it's critical that you clearly define your customer in specific terms.

- Every component in the Ideal-Future Vision step is important, as part of an overall, cohesive whole.

- The Ideal-Future Vision is necessary but not sufficient for success. You must go further with the full strategic plan, annual plan, and implementation and change.

IDEAL-FUTURE VISION

ACTION CHECKLIST

1. Develop a vision statement that is far-reaching and expresses your ideal future as an organization/business unit.

2. Create a mission statement that clearly identifies the who/what/why of your organization.

3. Make sure your vision and mission statements relate closely to the day-to-day realities of your organization.

4. As you shape your vision and mission statements, be certain that you keep your customer clearly defined and in focus.

5. Develop a set of core organizational values that you can adhere to, organization-wide, throughout the long-term.

6. Define your current organizational culture and the number of subculture levels throughout the organization.

7. Create an action plan that will help you shape a culture that is consistent throughout the organization.

8. Define your organization's driving force, so that you can develop an organization-wide, motivational rallying cry.

9. Make sure your organization's rallying cry contains the essence of your vision, mission, and values statements.

10. Assess the level of risk involved in making these changes . . . and take an honest inventory of your willingness to change.

KEY SUCCESS FACTORS/GOALS (STEP #3)

RECAP OF KEY POINTS

1. Be sure to reflect the customer's point of view, both internally and externally.

2. Measure all key elements of your Ideal-Future Vision.

3. Focus on outputs and results—except, possibly, for some crucial benchmarking on processes/systems.

4. Benchmarking vs. the competition may or may not be organization-wide Key Success Factors. However, at the business unit level of the organization, they definitely are Key Success Factors, and should be tracked and evaluated as such.

5. Be careful with competitive benchmarks; rarely do two firms in the same business sector function in exactly the same fashion.

6. Be sure to use the parallel process for Key Success Factors as well; ownership and buy-in are essential.

7. Cost/benefits analysis applies to their development, also. Use readily available data when at all possible.

8. If your vision should change at any point, remember to change your Key Success Factors accordingly.

9. Key Success Factors are often something new; it may take a year or so to get used to working with them and to get just the right measurement. Consider them cast in sand at first, and concrete later. So, don't publicly broadcast the exact targets too soon.

10. Some Key Success Factors like performance improvements are a long-term process; just tracking and measuring in the first year is an accomplishment. Have patience.

(continued)

KEY SUCCESS FACTORS/GOALS (STEP #3)

RECAP OF KEY POINTS *(concluded)*

11. Tie your executive bonus/incentive pay and rewards to Key Success Factors. This might be a separate project, but it is vitally important to success.

12. All performance appraisal forms should be tied to your core values (behaviors), as well as to the KSFs/strategies (results).

13. Since these factors are outcomes/results, they are often seen as goals or objectives, and the words can sometimes be used interchangeably. Be clear on your terms.

KEY SUCCESS FACTORS/GOALS

ACTION CHECKLIST

1. Determine your Key Success Factors/Goal areas, based on vision/values/mission and driving force(s). Do it first individually, then in subgroups, then the total group.

2. Set specific KSF factors and measures (targets) for the end-of-planning horizon (i.e., the year 2005), the baseline year (current year), and even intermediate targets, if possible. (If you don't have enough time, do these later, but do them—set a deadline.)

3. Assign KSF accountability for each KSF, and also an overall KSF Coordinator for total accountability to collect/report the data.

4. Evaluate your KSFs to make certain they are outputs/results/core values, vs. means-to-an-end. (Means should only be used when ends can't be measured effectively or the means are absolutely essential.)

5. Define/agree on priorities for the KSFs (i.e., forced ranking of 10 or less).

6. Eliminate the lowest priority KSFs if they are not critical or if you have too many (10 is maximum).

7. If you do not currently have the measure in place, your target for the first year will be to set it up and establish it on an ongoing basis.

8. Wherever possible, be sure to benchmark your KSFs against your competitors' best practices.

9. Set up the reporting format for KSFs and use it to track ongoing target vs. actual progress.

10. Establish a measurement to find out whether the plan and the total strategic management system has become a practical reality . . . just like a yearly independent financial audit.

CURRENT-STATE ASSESSMENT (STEP #4)

RECAP OF KEY POINTS

- When conducting your internal and external assessments, be willing to honestly accept all findings, not just the positive ones.

- In your internal Current-State Assessment, be sure to include thorough evaluation of these ten points:
    1. organization financial analysis
    2. core values analysis
    3. Key Success Factor analysis
    4. organization design
    5. business process reengineering
    6. management/leadership
    7. key human resource areas
    8. reward for total performance
    9. teamwork
    10. core competencies

- In your external Current-State Assessment, be sure to include evaluation of these ten areas:
    1. stakeholder analysis
    2. organizational life cycle
    3. industry structure analysis
    4. competitor analysis
    5. Strategic Business Unit (SBU) information
    6. customer focus
    7. market orientation and segmentation
    8. value map of products and services (positioning)
    9. market share and growth rate
    10. product/market certainty

- Be sure to conduct a SWOT analysis (with action implications) as a summary

CURRENT-STATE ASSESSMENT

ACTION CHECKLIST

- Analyze your organizational/business unit finances and core values . . . evaluate them on their capacity to support your Ideal-Future Vision.

- Study your unit's design to determine if it will get you where you want to go.

- Evaluate your organizational processes from your customer's point of view.

- Make sure you have the management and leadership skills you'll need.

- Look at organizational reward systems, both financial and nonfinancial.

- In conducting your Current-State Assessment (CSA), it is best to do so utilizing cross-functional teams (or other key stakeholders) in order to get a full picture of your organization's current performance. Prior to starting the assessment, decide which assessment tasks you want to conduct, then set up cross-functional teams to do the actual work.

- Scrutinize the organizational/business unit's core competencies.

- Identify your external key stakeholders, and decide on your responses to them in order to stay focused on your Ideal-Future Vision.

- Analyze what phases your organizational and industry life cycles are currently in.

- Make an indepth analysis of your competition.

(continued)

CURRENT-STATE ASSESSMENT

ACTION CHECKLIST *(concluded)*

- Be able to explain why each of your units should continue to exist.

- In your market orientation analysis, make sure you're concentrating on your most profitable customer base. (Also, determine whether your organization is structured around customer-focused units.)

- Develop a Value Map of your products or services, and define their market position.

- Do an indepth analysis of your current market share, and define how much your future market share should be.

- Look closely at each product line; determine the implications or risks inherent in any changes you may make.

- Complete your internal and external Current-State Assessments with a Strengths, Weaknesses, Opportunities, Threats (SWOT) analysis.

CORE STRATEGY DEVELOPMENT (STEP #5)

RECAP OF KEY POINTS

- Your organization will need to develop a small number (3–7) of core strategies to bridge the gaps between your Ideal-Future Vision and your Current-State Assessment.

- When developing your strategies, consider these newer strategies:
  — Flexibility
  — Speed
  — Horizontally integrated products
  — Networks and alliances
  — Environmentally improved products
  — Mass customization
  — Commonization/simplification
  — Business process reengineering (BPR)
  — Organizational learning
  — Employee morale/benefits
  — Management and leadership practices
  — Roll-ups
  — Experiences
  — Value-Chain Management

- There are five generic core strategy areas you need to consider:
  — Product-driven strategies
  — Market-driven strategies
  — Financial-driven strategies
  — Uniquely-driven strategies
  — Employee-driven strategies

- In order to successfully reinvent your strategic planning and implementation process, you must make accommodations for the Rollercoaster of Change we have described in this Guide.

(continued)

CORE STRATEGY DEVELOPMENT (STEP #5)

RECAP OF KEY POINTS *(concluded)*

- Also, be sure you integrate "building" as well as "cutting" (i.e., financial only) strategies . . . Remember, you've got to "play to win!"

- Have corresponding Strategic Action Items, prioritized over the next 12 months, for each of your core strategies.

- Create Strategy Sponsorship Teams that will champion each core strategy.

CORE STRATEGY DEVELOPMENT

ACTION CHECKLIST

- Make certain your vision/mission/core values and your Current-State Assessment (including SWOT) are final. Then develop your new core strategies.

- Develop a small number (3–7) of core strategies for implementing your organization's strategic plan. Make sure they serve you in the following ways:

  1. They should define your competitive business advantages, leading to long-term, sustainable organizational viability.

  2. They should help you select how you define, organize, and grow your Strategic Business Units (SBUs), including which SBUs your organization should create, retain, or eliminate.

  3. Core strategies should help you determine your overall organization design and structure, along with individual job design, employee initiatives, and philosophy.

  4. Core strategies should act as the "glue" for your yearly objectives, around which you'll organize your annual planning process.

- Develop core strategies that accommodate change, including cutting and building strategies. Don't be afraid to be very specific, indicating exactly what you're changing to, and exactly what you're changing from.

- Make sure your organization has clarity of any "from–to" paradigm shifts that will result from your new core strategies.

- Finalize your firm's driving force and Key Success Factors.

(continued)

CORE STRATEGY DEVELOPMENT

ACTION CHECKLIST *(concluded)*

- Develop cross-functional teams of change agents—we call them Strategy Sponsorship Teams—led by senior management. Also, assign a senior member of the core planning team to "champion" each core strategy (preferably a volunteer).

- Each strategy should have its own Strategic Action Items (SAIs), to be carried out over the life of the planning horizon. Once SAIs have been agreed upon, set the 3–5 top action priorities for each strategy over the next 12 months. If you have six core strategies with three top priorities each, you'll have a total of 18 top priority actions ("Must Do's").

- As soon as you've finished your list of top priority actions, make a list from this of actions to be taken in the next week, month, or quarter . . . Do NOT sacrifice the implementation of your new strategic plan to hesitation, confusion, or inaction!

- Finally, remember to take each strategic stage through a Parallel Process, giving all levels of your organization's workforce the opportunity to buy into the plan.

THREE-YEAR BUSINESS PLANNING (STEP #6)

RECAP OF KEY POINTS

- Evaluate your SBUs/MPAs to determine if any are outside your driving force(s) and core strategies/competencies.

- Identify which SBUs/MPAs need to change or be added in order to fulfill your organizational mission statement.

- Make sure you know the risk involved . . . and have specific plans to deal with it.

- Coordinate every step of your SBU/MPA planning to organization-wide core strategies.

- Limit your new business development searches to no more than 15–20% of your total effort and resources.

- In your 3-year Business Unit Planning, be sure to use the same systems thinking A-B-C-D phase process as was used during overall strategic planning.

- Incorporate new product development in your business unit planning.

- Identify the market segmentation of each business unit planning or service, and develop support strategies that include the four P's of marketing.

- Be sure to accommodate the support needs of each SBU/MPA business plan.

THREE-YEAR BUSINESS PLANNING

ACTION CHECKLIST

1. Define the units that currently exist in your organization.

2. Define the present revenue/profitability expectations of each.

3. Delineate the desired future of each unit, along with their future revenue/profits at the end of your planning horizon (Year "X").

4. Develop selection or exclusion criteria for SBU or MPA selection/exclusion/dropping . . . especially the customer/market research.

5. Analyze each unit based on that criteria; incorporate some traditional analysis tools as well (i.e., risk/focus/etc.).

6. Force-rank a set of priorities of the remaining units.

7. Analyze these decisions from a holistic perspective . . . make sure you haven't lost any core competencies by selective individual decisions.

8. For those units dropped or excluded, make a choice to either say "no" to the customer—or develop strategic alliances/partnerships with others to provide for them.

9. Establish goals/targets for overall organization growth (rates of volume and profitability, etc.).

10. Establish an ongoing system to manage the changes resulting from your prioritization.

11. Develop product/market plans, organization structure, teams, and budgets to achieve your unit targets . . . then adjust or repeat this cycle where necessary to match resources with targets.

ANNUAL PLANS AND STRATEGIC BUDGETS (STEP #7)

RECAP OF KEY POINTS

- To develop an effective annual plan, you need to make sure everyone focuses on organization-wide core strategies, not on separate department or turf issues.

- Make sure your actions for each core strategy support the top priority strategic action items identified by senior management.

- In the large-group review, your collective leadership should compare all annual plans against your vision, mission, values, strategies, and Key Success Factors.

- During the budget process, allocate funds based on how important the action is to achieving broad goals. Avoid department power struggles.

- It's important to study and evaluate various proactive approaches to reallocating your organization's funds.

- Before you cut costs in order to eliminate waste, you need to first define what waste is to you. Waste is anything other than the minimum amount of equipment, people, materials, parts, space, overhead, and work-time essential for added-value in your products or services.

- When seeking structural changes to do business at a lower costs, don't look only in the "now"—project into the future and consider possibilities from all angles.

- Organizations in the public sector are now looking for ways to be more proactive and raise money themselves—rather than waiting for funding.

- Be sure you have both a performance management system and a rewards and recognition system in place for employee motivation and commitment to your plan.

- In moving from planning to implementation, create a sense of ownership among employees (i.e., a rallying cry contest).

ANNUAL PLANS AND STRATEGIC BUDGETS

ACTION CHECKLIST

1. Prioritize Strategic Action Items under each strategy; use your core strategies as the organizing principles of your annual plans.

2. Develop departmental annual plans; include all senior department heads.

3. Have your collective leadership (your top 30–50 people) actively participate in a large-group annual plan review and problem-solving meeting.

4. Your top executives (i.e., CEO, President, COO, Executive Director, Superintendent, etc.) should present personal leadership plans spelling out what tasks they will personally do to help guide implementation.

5. At the close of your Large-Group Review, be sure that each participant prepares and presents one or two quick, easy actions for each strategy that they will take over the next two weeks.

6. Review and adopt some of the 10 ways to establish your approach to budgeting and resource allocation.

7. Design a performance management system that enables individuals to set goals based on the strategic plan—as well as to take accountability and responsibility for their part in the overall plan.

8. Create a rewards and recognition system that reinforces employee commitment and rewards contribution—while encouraging individual success with specific, tangible rewards and/or recognition.

9. Bridge the gap from planning to implementation by holding an organization-wide "rallying cry" contest.

PLAN-TO-IMPLEMENT (STEP #8)

RECAP OF KEY POINTS

- At the completion of your strategic/business planning, have a "Plan-to-Implement" Day with two segments: Executive Briefing and Educating; and Organizing Change Tasks.

- Know the difference between simply surviving change, and mastering change; develop viable change mechanisms you control over the long term.

- The first cardinal rule of change is that organizations don't change . . . people do.

- The second cardinal rule of change is that you must design and develop structures for managing change that are separate from existing, day-to-day organizational structures.

- If your top management doesn't set aside the time to manage and lead your change effort . . . it won't go far. Employees watch what you do—and what you don't do—for clues to your real priorities.

- You must prepare for and be ready to consistently manage the four phases in the Rollercoaster of Change because people change at different rates and speeds. The phases are (1) shock and denial, (2) depression, (3) hope, and (4) rebuilding.

- In order for your change effort to succeed, understand that your organization is a living, breathing system; use the "Organization-as-a-System" model to ensure fit, alignment, and integrity.

- When initiating the implementation of your strategic/business plan, be sure to incorporate all ten key change management factors or tasks:

(continued)

PLAN-TO-IMPLEMENT (STEP #8)

RECAP OF KEY POINTS *(concluded)*

1. Strategic plan rollout
2. Strategic Change Leadership Steering Committee
3. Internal support network
4. Allocate resources for change
5. Yearly comprehensive map of implementation
6. Strategy Sponsorship Teams
7. Key Success Factor tracking
8. Personal Leadership Plans
9. Performance and rewards system
10. Build the necessary support for change (critical mass)

- It is a critical senior management task to check your change management system for its fit, alignment, and integrity to your vision, on a constant basis.
- Conduct yearly recycling of your strategic plan.
- Conduct a yearly follow-up and diagnose overall implementation performance.

PLAN-TO-IMPLEMENT

ACTION CHECKLIST

1. Develop an initial rollout and communications plan.

2. Establish an organization-wide annual plan reflecting the strategic planning priorities for the first year.

3. Align the budget to reflect the strategic/business planning priorities.

4. Build all department/division/unit annual plans around the organization-wide annual priorities or goals.

5. Set up an ongoing Strategic Change Leadership Steering Committee to manage the change process.

6. Establish a yearly map—or master work plan—for 12-month implementation and follow-up. It should include 3-year business plans for any units or major support departments without these plans.

7. Establish a Key Success Factor monitoring, tracking, and reporting system.

8. Revise your performance and reward system to support your new vision, core strategies, and values.

9. Put an environmental scanning system in place—both yearly and in quarterly Strategic Change Leadership Steering Committee meetings (SKEPTIC).

10. Make sure top management takes an ongoing, active leadership role in your change process.

11. Build an internal support cadre with the expertise and skills to coordinate the strategic plan's implementation and change management.

12. Make sure key Strategy Sponsorship Teams are set up to build a critical mass for change.

STRATEGY IMPLEMENTATION AND CHANGE (STEP #9)

RECAP OF KEY POINTS

- In the Systems Thinking Approach, all Strategic Management is conducted within the four A,B,C,D phases of the systems model:

  Phase A—Future outcomes—Where do we want to be?

  Phase B—Feedback—How will we know when we get there?

  Phase C—Today's input—Where are we now, and what strategies should guide us?

  Phase D—Throughput actions—How do we get there?

- And Phase E—What is/might change in the environment?

- In systems thinking, you always, always focus on the outcomes—especially the key outcome of serving your customers.

- There are six specific ways in which you can apply the four-phase Systems Thinking Approach to Strategic Management:

  1. Comprehensive strategic planning

  2. Strategic Planning Quick (SPQ)

  3. Business unit planning

  4. Micro strategic planning

  5. Strategic change projects

  6. Strategic life planning

- Public sector organizations are finding that they experience many of the same problems that face the private sector, and are beginning to use a business orientation and a systems approach to their planning.

(continued)

STRATEGY IMPLEMENTATION AND CHANGE (STEP #9)

RECAP OF KEY POINTS *(concluded)*

- When public sector firms take a business thinking approach, they will have to deal with contradictions in areas such as these:
    — their mandate vs. their mission
    — lack of a profit motive
    — politicians on Board of Directors
    — lack of a customer focus
    — no measurements of success
    — parallel process = public consultation
    — low risk leadership styles
    — perceived resource constraints
    — lack of staff support for strategic management
    — ineffective change management

CHANGE MANAGEMENT FAIL-SAFE MECHANISMS

44 CHECKS AND BALANCES

Instructions: Review this list and make sure you've implemented all those that you need to. *Note*: * denotes the "must do's" that are essential to success. Actually, the more of these you set up, the higher your probability of successful implementation.

Do we have these?

Yes, No, or NI (needs improvement)

_____ *1. Plan-to-Plan/executive briefing (first), and "Engineer Success"—three goals of a Strategic Management System

_____ *2. Parallel Process throughout the planning and implementation process (key stakeholder involvement)
— buy in; stay in
— build critical mass for change, especially middle management

_____ *3. Three-Part Strategic Management System and Systems Thinking—*a new way to run your business*; the basics; an ongoing process

_____ *4. Vision—mission—core values statements in usable formats; customer-focused

_____ 5. Cultural/values audit and the creation of a culture change action plan—strategic change project

_____ *6. Core values placed on your performance appraisal form

_____ *7. Board of Directors involvement/ownership of the strategic plan; desire to use Key Success Factors for accountability; executive cooperation and regular status/communications to the Board

(continued)

161

CHANGE MANAGEMENT FAIL-SAFE MECHANISMS

44 CHECKS AND BALANCES *(continued)*

_____ 8. A crisp and clear single driving force and associated *rallying cry* that is the essence of your vision; it is the CEO's personal task to institutionalize this

_____ *9. Key Success Factor coordinator/support network and reporting system

_____ *10 Key Success Factor Continuous Improvement Matrix fully filled out with targets and measurements

_____ 11. Benchmarking against highly successful organizations (*best-practices* research)

_____ 12. Establishment of an Environmental Scanning System with specific accountability and feedback mechanisms

_____ 13. SWOT—staff involvement; reality check

_____ *14. Paradigm changes to strategies (from ➜ to) and a focused number of strategies

_____ *15. Strategic Sponsorship Teams set up for each core strategy

_____ *16. Core strategies also used as the Key Result Areas on performance appraisals

_____ *17. Annual planning format using strategies as *organizing framework* (the glue)
  — links to strategies
  — links to values, organizational and individual goal-setting/performance appraisals

_____ 18. Use of SBU *Pro Forma Matrix* to develop clear financial accountability

(continued)

CHANGE MANAGEMENT FAIL-SAFE MECHANISMS

44 CHECKS AND BALANCES *(continued)*

_____ *19. Three-year business planning for all business units to ensure clear competitive strategies; three-year business planning for Major Support Units also (by strategies)—WIIFM (especially a strategic plan for people-management)

_____ 20. Strategic business unit definition to lead organization design philosophy and efforts, focused on the businesses we are in … the customers we serve … and the employees we empower to do their best

_____ 21. Development of a priority maintenance system to handle interruptions/new ideas and lack of focus on strategies, business, and product development

_____ *22. Large-group annual planning review meeting (critique/sharing)

_____ 23. Strategic Change Project Teams for big, cross-functional ideas

_____ *24. Personal leadership plans/commitments developed by the CEO and top three executives of the organization

_____ 25. *War room* with all the changes and time-tables on the wall

_____ 26. Contingency planning; *what if* scenarios on key probable events

_____ *27. Annual planning and priority-setting first to drive the budgeting process (top three actions per each core strategy); looking at alternative ways to gain funds

_____ *28. One day offsite: Plan-to-Implement/Executive Briefing on *Change Process*

(continued)

163

CHANGE MANAGEMENT FAIL-SAFE MECHANISMS

44 CHECKS AND BALANCES *(continued)*

_____ *29. *Mastering Strategic Change* Workshop—simulation taught to all management personnel for indepth understanding of change management

_____ *30. Install different structures for change management, including Strategic Change Leadership Steering Committee (SCLSC) to guide:
—strategic plan implementation
—all change of any nature
The goal is *system alignment, attunement, and integrity.*

_____ *31. Annual comprehensive map on processes and structures required over next 12-month period for change management

_____ *32. Internal coordinator/facilitator and support network to support senior management

_____ 33. Create a critical mass action plan to support the vision, with ongoing communications planned throughout— use the Rollercoaster of Change concept

_____ *34. A rollout/communications strategy plan and reinforcement materials (PR/HR-led)

_____ 35. *Organization-as-a-System* framework (Organizational Systems Model); diagnosis and a way to ensure *system alignment and integrity* to the Strategic Plan—use the Wheel of Detail concept

_____ *36. Individual goals set by all exempt employees tied to the Strategic Plan . . . then use and model a true performance management system as a way to manage individual performance—part of HR strategic planning (the people-edge)

(continued)

CHANGE MANAGEMENT FAIL-SAFE MECHANISMS

44 CHECKS AND BALANCES *(concluded)*

_____ *37. A rewards diagnosis and improvement plan so that your rewards support the strategic direction (financial and nonfinancial)

_____ *38. Set up an Executive Development committee or board to manage promotions, executive hiring, and succession plan, as well as development and training

_____ *39. Creating customer value through business process reengineering action plan—strategic change project

_____ *40. Professional management and leadership practices (strategic leadership development system) action plan—strategic change project

_____ 41. Quarterly follow-up meetings with the Committee, all departments for all employees; focus on vision, key strategies, and rewards/celebrations

_____ *42. Organization and job redesign and restructuring action plan to be more customer-focused—strategic change project

_____ *43. Creating customer value through total quality/service action plan—strategic change project

_____ *44. Annual strategic review and update (like an independent financial audit and update) of the Strategic Plan next year's priorities

*These are **crucial** *fail-safe mechanisms*!

ENSURE SUCCESSFUL IMPLEMENTATION

Ten Key Meetings, Events, Training Programs, and Structures

1. Visionary Leadership Practices training — senior management and middle/first-line managers

2. Mastering Strategic Change training—senior management and middle/first-line managers

3. Strategic Change Leadership Steering Committee—meeting bimonthly

4. Weekly Executive Committee meetings/quarterly employee development committee meetings

5. Strategy sponsorship teams and parallel process meetings with key stakeholders

6. Internal cadre support—regular meetings

7. Teamwork and cross-functional team building training and development—all levels

8. Plan-to-implement meeting

9. Operational planning, large-group annual review meetings, and a strategic budgeting process

10. Annual Strategic Review and Update

Ten Big Change Project Tasks

1. Communications/rollout of the strategic plan

2. Key Success Factor development, tracking, and reporting

3. Performance Management Improvement

4. Rewards and appraisals revamped

5. Total Service Management/customer-focused organization-wide

6. TQM for all products/organizational-wide, as well

7. Annual strategic assessment

8. Organization redesign and restructuring

9. Blow out bureaucracy and waste

10. Build a total succession—career—management development system

CONCLUSION

IX. Facilitation Tips

KEY TIPS ON FACILITATING CLOSURE IN EXECUTIVE GROUPS

1. Set up ground rules in the beginning; especially consensus = active support.

2. Have a one-to-one conversation with the CEO about the amount of participation and participative management required.

3. Get closure by being focused and disciplined. Restrict the discussions to one topic at a time. (List all topics on a flip chart.)

4. Get closure on easy topics first to get positive movement and to isolate the difficult issues until last.

5. Wait to talk or intervene until people start repeating their ideas—i.e., saying the same thing or "going around the barn" a second time.

6. Test for closure—"I may be wrong, but are you saying that . . ?"

7. Take a neutral position; help people get answers that make sense or seem logical for them.

8. Getting closure is the goal—be nonjudgmental/neutral as to what it is.

9. Stay above the debate; don't get caught up in it.

10. Often it is best to just sit and observe for ten minutes or more. Let them discuss and frame the issues; you just actively listen.

11. Follow where the energy takes them—passion vs. logic. Passion is great in support of the decision, but be sure logic backs it up. Be a devil's advocate; ask "dumb" questions.

12. Randomly write down logic patterns on a flip chart; often the answer emerges.

13. Don't skip over resistance. Go into it by asking *why?*—Have individuals explain the logic/rationale behind their opinion.

14. Your job is to make it easy for the group to focus and talk openly. Protect the minority point of view.

15. Impartiality is key. When you have a bias, turn it into an open-ended question instead.

16. Too much content expertise can be a liability, as can too much commitment to the organization. Be calm, centered, neutral.

17. Come back later to reaffirm and solidify/clarify the earlier decision (two consensus checks)—i.e., sleep on it!

18. Root out hidden agendas: Ask "Why?" up to five times.

19. Influence often goes to whoever has the last word.

20. Ask them to collaborate on reaching consensus closure; you can't do it alone. In the extreme: "If you don't focus on closure, why should I? It's your meeting."

21. Go around the room to give everyone a chance to be heard. Closure often emerges as you do this.

22. Even the CEO must share the logic of his/her opinions and decisions. Is he/she willing to listen, be naive, learn, and be wrong?

23. Achieving "premature slam-dunk shutdowns" instead of working to closure is the novice's worst move. Only the group has this decision. Instead of shutting down differences prematurely, ask permission for shut down (along with next-steps and when to finish closure). You can also give advance signals/comments that time is about up and ask for help with the process/next-steps/closure.

Index

AM/PM Mini Marts, 78
Analytic thinking, 22
Annual department plans, 104
Annual plans, 9, 38, 89–92, 126
    action checklist, 155
    format, 92, 129
    recap, 154
Annual strategic review, 10–11,
    123–124, 129
Apple, 66, 78

The Balanced Scorecard, 52
Banff Center for Management, 117
Benchmarking, 104, 142
Best-practices research,
    high-performance work
    organization, 76
BFI, 78
Boeing, 68
Briefings, 32, 40, 93, 125, 136, 138,
    156
Budget(s), 9, 89–92
    action checklist, 155
    cuts, 27, 80
    recap, 154
Business plan, 8–9, 107
    customizing, 36–39
    developing, 29–35, 40
Business planning, 85–88. *See also*
    Strategic planning; Three-year
    business planning
    reinventing, 133–135
    vs. strategic planning, 24, 56
Business process reengineering, 5,
    27, 48, 61, 80
Business processes, 67–68
Buy-in, 12, 14, 106

Cascade of planning, (illus.) 87–88,
    91
Centre for Strategic Management,
    130
CEO, role in strategic change, 112,
    117–118
Change, 26
    implementation of, 116–122
    leadership and, 6–11
    reality of, 1–2
Change efforts, reasons for failure,
    96–101
Change management, fail-safe
    mechanisms, 161–165
Change process, 70
Choice, 50
Coach, 120
Competitive edge, 50
Comprehensive map, 10, 107, 124
Consultants, external, 32–34, 99,
    123
Core strategies, 61, 63, 77–84, 108,
    118, 128
Core strategy development
    action checklist, 150–151
    recap, 148–149
Core values, 42, 43, 62
    assessment, 71–72
Cost/benefits analysis, 142
Cross-functional teams, 68, 99
Cultural diversity, 100
Current-state assessment, 9, 55–58
    action checklist, 146–147
    assessment areas, 57–58
    recap, 145
Customer focus, 15–18, 26, 118
    assessment, 16–17
    systems thinking and, 48–50

Customer satisfaction, 1, 52, 59–60
Customer value, 10
    creating, (illus.) 7, 50, 60,
        (illus.) 95, 123
Customer-focus organization, 36,
  44
Customer(s), defining, 41

Daimler-Chrysler, 67, 77
Delivery, 38–39
Drucker, Peter, 117

Educational briefing, 93
Employee Development Board, 103
Employee satisfaction, 1, 52
Empowerment, 87
Environment, 18, 63
Environmental scanning, 32, 110
Excellence, 69
Executive briefing, 32, 40, 125,
  136, 138, 156
Executive Committee, 103
External consultants, 32–34, 35, 99,
  123
Exxon, 68

Facilitation tips, 167–168
Facilitator, 120
Feedback, 18, 62
Feedback loop, 51–53, 60
Financial viability, 52
Ford, 117
Future, 1–2
    ideal, 19

General Electric (G.E.), 66, 68, 77
General Motors (GM), 68, 117–118
General systems theory (GST), 17–
  18, (illus.) 20, 59
Giant Industries, 59, 73, 77, 87
GM. *See* General Motors
Goals, 1–2

Gorbachev, Mikhail, 106
Government, core strategies, 79.
    See also Public sector
    organizations
GST. *See* General systems theory

Haines Associates model, 59
Hard Rock Café, 78
High performance, 3–4
    creating and sustaining, 10–11
    sustaining, 123–124
High-performance organization
  survey, 75
High-performance work
  organization, 76
Human resource management
  systems, 10, 119, 128

IBM, 68
Iceberg theory of change (illus.),
  93–96
Ideal future, 29–40
Ideal-future vision, 8–9, 41–50
    action checklist, 141
    recap, 140
Imperial Corporation of America,
  60
Implementation, 3–4, 9–10, 63, 64
    meetings, events, training
      programs, 166
    plan-to-implement, 93–115
    recap, 159–160
    strategy implementation and
      change, 116–122
In Search of Excellence, 48
Input, 18, 60–63
Internal communications
  coordinator, 112
Internal staff change management
  coordinator, 112
Internal staff facilitator, 112

Kaizen, 68
Key stakeholders, 14, 27
Key success factor continuous
    improvement matrix, 53
Key success factor coordinator, 112
Key success factors (KSFs), 8, 51–
    53, 62, 129, 154, 158
        action checklist, 144
        recap, 142–143
Kieretsus, 66, 78
KISS method, 84, 107
Kroc, Ray, 48
KSFs. *See* Key success factors

Large-group review meeting, 89,
    129, 155
Large-scale organizational change
    (illus.), 105
Lawlor, Ed, 129
Leadership, 10, 103, 118
        competencies, 13
        visionary, 12–13
Leadership practices workshop, 126
Living Systems, 23
Living systems, 23–24

Major program areas (MPAs), 9, 85,
    (illus.) 86, 151
Management, managing change
    and, 6–11
        resistance by, 97
Marriott, J. W., 48
McDonald's, 48
Measurement and benchmarking
    team, 104
Meetings
        implementation, 166
        large-group review, 89, 129,
            155
Micro strategic planning, 8, 159
Microsoft, 66, 78
Middle manager skills, 99

Miller, James G., 23
Mission, 43, 62, 140, 141
Mission statement, 41
Mission-development triangle
    exercise, 45
MPAs. *See* Major program areas

Nissan, 78
No-Excuses Management, 96
Nordstrom, 48

Operational indicators, 52
Operational planning, 9, 63
Organization, as a system, 18,
    (illus.) 65
        model, 10, 59–70, 119, 156
        organizational culture and,
            69–74
Organization design, 119
Organization structure, 66
Organizational culture, 8
        changing, 70
        organization as system and,
            69–74
Organizational values exercise, 46–
    47
Outcome measures, 8, 26, 51–53,
    60
Outcomes, 15–18
Output, 18, 62
Ownership, of plan, 12, 14

Pacific Gas & Electric, 108
Parallel process, 8, (illus.) 12–14,
    128, 142, 151
Participative management, 98
Partnerships, 66
Performance appraisal, 91, 142
Performance management system,
    91, 155
Personal leadership plans, 107
Peters, Tom, 48

Planning team, 12–14
Plan-to-implement, 9–10, 126
    action checklist, 158
    recap, 156–157
Plan-to-implement day, 107–108
Plan-to-plan, 8, 32–34, 125
    action checklist, 138–139
    recap, 136–137
    tasks, 40
Plan-to-review, 123
Platform teams, 67, 68
Positioning, 43, 50, 118
Proactive organizations, 60
Professionalism, 119–122
Public sector organizations, 154,
    159–160
    core strategies, 79
Public-private partnerships, 67

Quality, 50

Rainforest Café, 78
Rallying cry, 42, 43, 140, 141, 154,
    155
Reactive organizations, 60, 66
Recognition, 91
Reinforcements, 96
Renewals (illus.), 81
Reorganization, 80
Resource allocation, 89–92. *See
    also* Budgets
Responsiveness, 50
Reward systems, 91, 146, 154
Rodgers, T. J., 96
Rollercoaster of change, (illus.) 81,
    102, 105–106, 118, 148, 156

SBUs. *See* Strategic business units
Senior management
    modeling, 99
    role in strategic management,
      130

Service, 50
Shared vision statement, 41
Six Sigma, 68
SKEPTIC, 63, 99, 136, 158
SPOTS syndrome, 6, 25, 107
SSTs. *See* Strategy Sponsorship
    Teams
Star results, 38, 49–50, 60, 124, 128
Status quo, 33, 97
Stay-in, 106
Strategic budgets, 89–92. *See also*
    Budgets
Strategic business units (SBUs), 9,
    37–38, 85, (illus.) 86, 150, 152,
    159
Strategic change, 117–122
    projects, 159
    structures and roles, 103–104
Strategic Change Leadership
    Steering Committee, 10, 73, 103,
    105, 107, 116, 126, 128, 158, 166
    agenda, 113–114, 116
    annual strategic review and,
      123–124
    roles, 112
Strategic life planning, 159
Strategic management
    beginning, 125–131
    benefits, 26–28
    common mistakes, 25, 133–
      134
    implementation tips, 127–131
    levels of living systems, 23–
      24
    phases, (illus.) vii, 19–22
    ten-step model (illus.), 30
Strategic management
    system,(illus.) 28, 130
    goals, 2–3
    yearly cycle, 115
Strategic plan, 3–4, 8–9, 107
    customizing, 36–39

Strategic plan *(continued)*
        developing, 29–35, 40
Strategic planning, 6–11, 60–63,
    (illus.) 81. *See also* Business
    planning
            vs. business planning, 24, 56
            common mistakes, 25
            conducting, 8–9
            customizing, 37–39, 126–127
            reinventing, 133–135
Strategic planning quick, 8, 159
Strategy development, 77–84
Strategy implementation, 116–122
        recap, 159–160
Strategy Sponsorship Teams
    (SSTs), 10, 83–84, 103, 108,
    112, 123, 128, 149, 151, 158
Sunoco, 66
Support departments, 85
        operational planning and, 9
Support staff, 32–34, 103, 110, 128
        duties, 35
Support systems, 39
SWOT analysis, 55, 124, 145, 147,
    150
Systems
        defined, 19
        living, 23–24
Systems thinking approach, (illus.)
    viii, 2–4, 15–18, 21–22
        customer focus, 15–18, 48–50
        model (illus.), 20
        phases, 59–65
        strategic management cycle
            and system, 5–11
        visionary leadership practices,
            12–14

Teams, 38, 67, 68, 99. *See also*
    Strategic Change Leadership
    Steering Committee; Strategy
    Sponsorship Teams

Teamwork, 26, 39
Technology Steering Committee,
    103
Three-year business planning, 8, 9,
    12–13, 85. *See also* Business
    planning; Strategic planning
        action planning, 153
        model (illus.), 31
        recap, 152
Three-year business unit plans, 77
Throughput, 18, 63, 64
Total cost, 50
Total quality management (TQM),
    5, 27, 48, 61, 66, 117, 166
        strategic planning and, 62–63
Toyota, 77, 78
TQM. *See* Total quality
    management
Traditional organizations, 60
Trainer, 120
Training programs, 166
Turn-arounds (illus.), 81

*The Ultimate Advantage:
    Creating the High Involvement
    Organization,* 129

Value chain management, 5, 48, 78
Value map, 147
Values, organizational, 46–47
Vision, 1–2, 43, 62, 69, 127, 140,
    141. *See also* Ideal-future vision

Waste, 154
Welch, Jack, 66
WorkOut, 68

Year #1 strategic change process
    checklist, 107–111
Yearly Comprehensive Map, 10,
    107, 124

Yearly cycle, strategic management
   system, 115
Yearly strategic management cycle,
   6, (illus.) 28
Yearly update, 39. *See also* Annual
   strategic review
Yeltsin, Boris, 107

ABOUT THE AUTHOR

Stephen G. Haines has used systems thinking as his orientation to life since the late 1970s. He is currently president and founder of the Centre for Strategic Management® and an internationally recognized leader in strategic planning and strategic change. He has over 25 years of diverse international executive and consultant experience in virtually every part of both the private and public sectors.

Mr. Haines was formerly president and part owner of University Associates (UA) Consulting and Training Services. Prior to that, he was executive vice president and chief administrative officer of Imperial Corporation of America, a $13 billion nationwide financial services firm. He has been on eight top management teams with organization leadership for operations, planning, human resources, training, organization development, marketing, sales, communications, public relations, and facilities.

A 1968 U.S. Naval Academy (at Annapolis) engineering graduate with a foreign affairs minor, Mr. Haines has an Ed.D. (ABD) in management and educational psychology from Temple University and an M.S. in organization development from George Washington University.

Steve has written six books and eight volumes of the Centre's took kits, guides, and best practices (over 4000 pages), all based on systems thinking. He has taught over 60 different types of seminars and is in demand as a keynote speaker on CEO and Board of Directors issues. He has served on a number of boards and was chairman of the board for Central Credit Union in San Diego.

The Centre for Strategic Management® is an unusual mix of 12 master-level partners in the United States and Canada, with a growing number of master-consultant international affiliates in Australia, Korea, Turkey, South Africa, and Ireland.